Exodus
and
Wanderings

LESSONS FROM THE OLD TESTAMENT
VOLUME 2

Jonathan Turner

ഇൽ

ഇൻൽ

Table of Contents

Introduction...1

1   Preparing a New Leader.................................5

2   A Reluctant Leader.......................................10

3   Let My People Go!..16

4   With a Mighty Hand......................................24

5   Crossing the Sea...31

6   Trusting Daily...37

7   Covenant Codified..45

8   Highlights of the Law...................................54

9   Sacrifices and Festivals................................62

10 The Tabernacle...68

11 Covenant Broken and Renewed...................76

12 Burdens of Leadership.................................81

13 Too Much of a Good Thing?........................88

14 Revolt in the Desert.....................................94

15 The End In Sight..99

16 The Donkey and the Seer...........................105

17 Blessings and Curses..................................110

    Appendix – Thoughts on the Exodus.........117

    Bibliography...128

    About the Author..129

ഇൻ

List of Illustrations

Layout of the Tabernacle..69

Probable Route of the Exodus...125

ഔങ

Introduction

What is a nation? According to the dictionary it is a people who speak the same language, have a common history, a common government and a defined territory. This definition is only partially correct. At least in ancient times, a nation did not necessarily have a defined territory. Some nations were nomadic and their territory, if any could be called their own, was ill-defined.

While a common history and the same language may bind people together, it is not enough to make a nation. Similarly, living under the same government is not necessarily what forms a nation. There have been many empires in history which contained distinct people groups who considered themselves nations within the empire.

What makes a nation is more than a common history and a common government. The people in a nation may be homogeneous or come from many different ethnic and cultural backgrounds. What binds them together is not their government, per se, but a common outlook, a shared ethic and world-view.

Perhaps even more important, a nation will have a sense of otherness. The people of a nation will consider that there is something about them which is unique. There is something which sets them apart from all other peoples or nations. Sometimes this sense of being different may cause a nation to feel superior to others or, it may make them feel inferior in some ways. Either way, they always consider themselves somehow distinct.

There is little doubt that the Israelite people became a nation, and thus developed their sense of otherness and uniqueness, during the time of their Exodus from Egypt and their wanderings before they conquered Canaan. (See Numbers 23:9.)

Before the Exodus the Israelites were already unique in that they were the heirs of the promises God had made to Abraham and the other patriarchs. Yet, they still shared many of the characteristics and, to an extent, even the same ancestry as other tribes and peoples around them. After the Exodus, no one could say that the Israelites were not a unique and different people.

What was it that made them unique and gave them their sense of otherness? Here is a very incomplete list:

> 1) God called and chose the Israelites over all other people (Deuteronomy 10:15).
>
> 2) God made a distinction between the Israelites and the Egyptians (Exodus 8:22-23, 9:4, 11:7).
>
> 3) God gave them a different calendar (Exodus 12:1-2).
>
> 4) God gave them different festivals (Exodus 12:14-20).
>
> 5) They were given a different pathology (Exodus 15:26).
>
> 7) God entered into a unique covenant with them (Exodus 19:3-6).
>
> 8) God gave them a different diet (Leviticus 11:1-47).
>
> 9) God told the Israelites not to copy the customs of other nations (Leviticus 20:23, Deuteronomy 18:9).

From the above list it is obvious that God fully intended the Israelites to be unique and different than everyone else. It was necessary for the Israelites to be separate from the other nations if they were to fulfill the role God had in mind for them in salvation history. God designated them as a nation of priests (Exodus 19:6). In other words, the Israelites were to be a channel of blessing and redemption to those around them. Specifically, it was through the Israelites that God would one day bring the Savior into the world. They could hardly fulfill that role if they did not remain a distinct, different and unique people.

There were times when the Israelites' sense of otherness and separateness was jeopardized. For example, hundreds of years after the Exodus, the Israelites demanded a king. Their request displeased both God and the prophet Samuel. It is unlikely that the concept of monarchy was the problem, for provisions for a king were part of the Mosaic Law right from the beginning (Deuteronomy 17:14-20). The problem seems to have been the motive for asking for a king: "Then we will be like all the other nations…" (1 Samuel 8:20 NIV)

Centuries later when the Israelites had largely succeeded in losing their unique identity by becoming like the other nations, God had to purge them through conquest and exile. However, regardless of the compromises of the nation at large, there was always a faithful remnant of people who never forgot their unique status as God's chosen. It was through them that the Messiah eventually came.

The concepts of otherness and separation are still important. The followers of Christ are unique and different than those around them. Jesus told His disciples, "If you belonged to the world, it would love you as its own. As it is, you do not belong to the world, but I have chosen you out of the world. That is why the world hates you." (John 15:19 NIV) Both the writer of Hebrews and the Apostle Peter echo the same idea. Those who are in covenant relationship with God are so different that they are aliens and strangers to those around them. (For example, see Hebrews 11:13 and 1 Peter 2:11.) They are citizens of a different country and are only temporary residents in this world (Philippians 3:20, Hebrews 11:14-16, 2 Peter 3:13).

Because Jesus' followers do not belong to this world, not only their actions, but their very thought patterns should be distinct from those who do not follow Him. The Apostle Paul wrote, "Therefore, I urge you, brothers, in view of God's mercy, to offer your bodies as living sacrifices, holy and pleasing to God – this is your spiritual act of worship. Do not conform any longer to the pattern of this world, but be transformed by the renewing of your mind. Then you will be able to test and approve what God's will is – his good, pleasing and perfect will." (Romans 12:1-2 NIV)

The otherness of Christians can not only be defined by what they are not, that is they are not of this world, but also by what they are in contrast to the world. Peter writes, "But you are a chosen people, a royal priesthood, a holy nation, a people belonging to God, that you may declare the praises of him who called you out of darkness into his wonderful light. Once you were not a people, but now you are the people of God; once you had not received mercy, but now you have received mercy." (1 Peter 2:9-10 NIV)

Interestingly enough, God used almost identical terms to "royal priesthood" and "holy nation" for the Israelites when they entered into covenant with Him (Exodus 19:5-6). This is one reason why the Exodus and period of wandering are still relevant to us today. Though the events took place over 3,000 years ago, we can still learn a great deal from them.

I have based lessons in this volume on the books of Exodus, Numbers, Leviticus and Deuteronomy.

೮೦೦೩

Preparing a New Leader
(Exodus 1:1-2:25)

Introduction: The book of Exodus marks a major milestone in salvation history. 400 years have passed since the events recorded at the end of Genesis. The 70 people who had migrated to Egypt from Palestine have turned into a group of several hundred thousand. In Genesis, God dealt with individuals who were the heads of families. That is why we call it the Patriarchal Age. But in Exodus, a change takes place. Instead of making covenants with individuals, God makes one with a nation.

What was the purpose of the covenants? During the Patriarchal Age, it was primarily to give hope. God promised that some day there would be a Savior. The message of hope is still present in the covenant God made with the nation of Israel, but there was another purpose for it as well. It was to demonstrate that no matter how hard we humans try on our own, we can never live up to the perfection God demands. He is holy and perfect, and if we are to live in His presence we, too, must be perfect. But we aren't able to meet the standard. One reason God made the covenant with the nation of Israel and gave them the Law of Moses was to teach us all our need for Christ. Paul writes, "Before this faith came, we were held prisoners by the law, locked up until faith should be revealed. So the law was put in charge to lead us to Christ that we might be justified by faith. Now that faith has come, we are no longer under the supervision of the law." (Galatians 3:23-25 NIV)

Before God could teach the lesson, though, He had to prepare both the nation and the man who would introduce the nation to the covenant.

I.   Joseph Forgotten (Exodus 1:1-14)

We humans tend to have short memories. We forget our history. Genesis 47:25 recounts that the Egyptians recognized that Joseph had saved them from starvation and were grateful to him. But when we get to Exodus, many years have passed. Exodus 1:8 records that a king came to power who did not know about Joseph. The Egyptians had forgotten their history and, along with it, their gratitude for what Joseph had done for the nation.

At the time Joseph and his family lived, Egypt was ruled by what are known as the Hyksos kings. They were from a tribe which was not originally from Egypt. They had migrated there and overthrown the previous dynasty. Though these newcomers had integrated themselves into Egyptian culture, the natives resented them. Eventually, after a few hundred years, they rebelled and drove the Hyksos out. The new king was of Egyptian descent. One reason for the hatred he displayed toward the Israelites may have been that, in his opinion, the Israelites were associated with the rulers he had thrown out.

II.   Population Control (Exodus 1:15-22)

How do you deal with a hated and feared people? Throughout history, mankind has come up with the same two depressing scenarios: First, oppress them. And, when that doesn't work, try to kill them off.

It seems we never learn. If you want population to decrease, don't oppress people. That's counterproductive. More kids are born to those who can't afford the means to prevent pregnancy. Instead make people prosperous. The richer people are, the fewer kids they tend to have.

There is a broader principle here. We all have people in our lives who give us trouble. Our natural tendency is respond in ways to hurt them. But the Bible teaches that we should do the opposite. "Do not repay anyone evil for evil. Be careful to do what is right in the eyes of everybody. If it is possible, as far as it depends on you, live at peace with everyone. Do not take revenge, my friends, but leave room for God's wrath, for it is written: "It is mine to avenge; I will repay," says the Lord. On the contrary: "If your enemy is hungry, feed him; if he is thirsty, give him something to drink. In doing this, you will heap burning coals on his head." Do not be overcome by evil, but overcome evil with good." (Romans 12:17-21 NIV)

The second phase of population control is to try to kill off the undesired population. In this case, the midwives were told to abort all male babies. The midwives disobeyed. As a result, God was kind to them (Exodus 1:20).

Application: This should tell us something about what God thinks of those who kill babies. In many cultures, abortion has become an accepted practice. But never forget that every time an abortion is performed, a life is killed. The taking of life is not something which God views lightly.

III.   Literal Obedience (Exodus 2:1-10)

Since the Egyptians couldn't trust the midwives to decrease the population through abortion, the next brilliant scheme was to tell parents they had to throw their baby boys into the Nile river. This was more than just a rather bizarre way to kill off boys. The Egyptians believed that the Nile was divine. They worshiped it. In reality, to throw the boys into the river was to sacrifice them to the river god. In other words, the Egyptians were not only trying to get rid of a portion of the population they didn't want, they were also trying to destroy the worship of the One True God.

In the face of what seemed impossible odds, one couple came up with a creative solution. Literal obedience. They obeyed the order to throw their baby into the river, but there was nothing that said he couldn't be in a boat! There's a real lesson here. When someone orders us to do something which is contrary to God's will, rather than outright defiance, we will often be better off to find a creative way to keep the letter of the law without disobeying God. Yes, there is a time when we have to disobey laws and take the consequences. But we should find other solutions if we can.

When we determine to honor God, He will honor our commitment to Him. In this case, not only was Moses' life spared, his mother got paid for taking care of him. This paved the way for one of the most remarkable educations in history.

IV.   Leadership Training (Exodus 2:11-22)

First, Moses was thoroughly trained as a Hebrew. He never forgot who his people were. Though he was raised as the son of Pharaoh's daughter, he identified himself as a Hebrew. Exodus 2:11 says that he went out to see his own people. This wasn't just a cultural thing. Somewhere along the line, Moses developed a deep and lasting faith in God. Hebrews 11:24-26 says, "By faith Moses, when he had grown up, refused to be known as the son of Pharaoh's daughter. He chose to be mistreated along with the people of God rather than to enjoy the pleasures of sin for a short time. He regarded disgrace for the sake of Christ as of greater value than the treasures of Egypt, because he was looking ahead to his reward." (NIV)

Secondly, Moses got a thorough Egyptian education. At this period of history, Egyptian education was the best in the world. As a royal prince, possibly even being groomed for the throne, Moses would have gotten the best of the best. Acts 7:22 says, "Moses was educated in all the wisdom of the Egyptians and was powerful in speech and action." (NIV)

In spite of his unique education, Moses still needed to learn a few things:

> 1) You have to rely on God's strength, not your own. He tried to take things into his own hands, and really made a mess of it. He ended up murdering a man. We all tend to do things in our own strength. We need to learn the lesson, "…'Not by might nor by power, but by my Spirit,' says the LORD Almighty." (Zechariah 4:6 NIV)

> 2) The timing has to be right. Moses wanted to rescue his people, but the people weren't yet ready for him to rescue them. It's hard to wait, but that is often what God asks us to do. "Be still before the LORD and wait patiently for him; do not fret when men succeed in their ways, when they carry out their wicked schemes. Refrain from anger and turn from wrath; do not fret – it leads only to evil." (Psalm 37:7-8 NIV)

> 3) Moses had to learn the lesson of humility. As a result of his rejection, Moses began to regard himself as a failure. Later, when God asked him to rescue the Israelites from slavery, Moses didn't think he was capable of doing it. He had to learn that people who have failed by relying on their

own strength, are victorious when they rely on God. He needed to learn that God can use even murderers.

Moses' education in Egypt lasted 40 years. The second half of his education lasted another 40 years. No doubt it must have seemed like wasted time to him. He gave up his dream. But God was preparing him all those years for the biggest task of his life.

Lesson: Don't give up, even when it seems like nothing is happening and all your dreams are shattered. God isn't done with you yet!

V.   God Hears (Exodus 2:23-25)

In the meantime, things had been going from bad to worse in Egypt. Finally, the people were ready to be freed from their slavery.

There are some important lessons here:

1) You have to want to be saved. At the time Moses had tried to save them, 40 years prior, they didn't want to be saved. They rejected Moses' leadership. This is one reason God allows hardship in our lives. It is to bring us to the place where we recognize the hopelessness of our situation and are ready to trust God for deliverance.

2) Just because you don't get an immediate answer, doesn't mean that God isn't listening. We get impatient when our prayers aren't answered in the next 5 minutes. But God often has been working on the answer to our problems for a long time, without us even being aware of it or what form the answer will take. God had been preparing the answer to the Israelites' cries for the last 80 years. Isaiah 65:24 says, "Before they call I will answer; while they are still speaking I will hear." (NIV)

෨෬

A Reluctant Leader
(Exodus 3:1-4:31)

Introduction: We humans have a tendency to go from one extreme to the other. If we find out that we are wrong in a particular area, it's easy to make as serious a mistake in the opposite direction. Though he was raised as Egyptian royalty, Moses never forgot his own people. It was his desire to deliver them from slavery. His problem was that he went about it the wrong way. Instead of relying on God, Moses took things into his own hands. It wasn't the right time, and Moses didn't use the right methods. As a result, his own people rejected his leadership. In addition, he murdered a man and was forced to flee Egypt.

Forty years pass. The time is now right for the Israelites' deliverance. But Moses has now swung to the opposite extreme. He not only doubts his own ability to lead, he also doubts God's ability to save His people.

I. Holy Ground (Exodus 3:1-6)

When and where do we encounter God?

> Most people seem to think that God is found only inside church buildings. But that isn't the case. God created the whole universe and He may be found anywhere. Another misconception people have is that we encounter God only when we set out to worship Him. But many, if not most, of the encounters with God which are recorded in the Bible, took place when people were going about their ordinary, every-day business. The question is: Are we ready to meet God at all times, in all places?

Another important question is, "What makes a place holy?"

> Most people would say that a place is holy if it has been set aside, or dedicated, to God. At best, that is only a partial truth. What really makes a place holy is God's presence. If God isn't there, even a chapel or a cathedral isn't holy. As

Moses found out, if God is there, even a patch of brush is holy.

Application: This concept, that it's the presence of God which makes a place holy, has a special meaning and application for Christians. We are repeatedly told that God lives in us through His Holy Spirit. For example, in Ephesians 2:21-22 it says, "In him the whole building is joined together and rises to become a holy temple in the Lord. And in him you too are being built together to become a dwelling in which God lives by his Spirit." (NIV) Now, if God lives in us we are, by definition, holy. We need to think and act in a way that is consistent with the holy status God has given us. "As obedient children, do not conform to the evil desires you had when you lived in ignorance. But just as he who called you is holy, so be holy in all you do; for it is written: "Be holy, because I am holy."" (1 Peter 1:14-16 NIV)

II.   God Is Not Indifferent (Exodus 3:7-10)

Does trouble mean that God is angry with us?

When we are going through hard times it's tempting to think that it's because we've done something wrong. Now, it's always a good thing to consider whether we're in trouble because we're reaping the consequences of our own sin. If we are, we need to repent and get things right. But don't forget that some of the trouble we encounter is the result of other people's sin. If we're not guilty, then we shouldn't wallow in false guilt. In this case, the Israelites were suffering, not because of what they had done, but because of the sin of the Egyptians. Exodus 3:9 clearly says that the Egyptians were oppressing them.

Does suffering mean that God doesn't care?

Not at all. In Exodus 3:7, God says that He was concerned. But if God cares, why doesn't He prevent suffering, or at least stop it right away? There are several possible reasons.

1) God's purpose in every situation and circumstance is to draw us closer to Himself and make us more like Christ. Sometimes suffering is the only way we will learn some of the lessons we need to make us more Christlike.

2) Sometimes, God waits to help us until we ask. James writes, "…You do not have, because you do not ask God. When you ask, you do not receive, because you ask with wrong motives, that you may spend what you get on your pleasures." (James 4:2-3 NIV)

3) Sometimes God allows suffering to continue, because the conditions aren't yet right to put an end to it. We tend to forget that we are not the only people in the world, and that our problems are not the only problems. God has to take, not only our problems but, everything else into account. In this specific case, God had promised the land of Canaan to the Israelites. But what about the people who were already living there? In Genesis 15:16, God told Abraham that the Israelites couldn't have the land until the sins of the people who were already there had reached a limit. God had to wait to bring relief to the Israelites until those people had crossed the line.

Lesson: Don't give up on God even though it seems like you are going through a lot of trouble. He cares. He will act when the time and circumstances are right.

III.   Excuses, Excuses (Exodus 3:11-4:17)

God was ready to act, but Moses wasn't. What excuses did he give?

1) Excuse No. 1: "Who am I?" (Exodus 3:11) Moses basically said that he wasn't qualified for the job. He wasn't capable of dealing with Pharaoh and he wasn't qualified to lead the people out of Egypt.

What was God's response?

God wasn't expecting Moses to do this by himself. He wasn't to depend on his own skills and qualifications. He'd already gotten himself into trouble by doing that. Instead, God promised to be with Moses (Exodus 3:12). If there was any doubt in Moses' mind that God was really calling him to do this task, those doubts would be removed by the fact that the Israelite nation would worship on the mountain where God was speaking to him.

2) Excuse No. 2: "They won't know that I represent You (Exodus 3:13). Right. Anybody can make a claim that he represents God. What do I tell them if they ask which God I'm representing?"

What was God's reply?

> a) Tell them that you represent the "I AM." This Name will ring true with what they know of My character (Exodus 3:14-15).
>
> b) Remind them of the promises I've made through the centuries to their ancestors (Exodus 3:16-17).
>
> c) Don't sweat it. They'll listen to you. I promise that I'll get you out of Egypt (Exodus 3:18-22).

3) Excuse No. 3: "They won't believe me." (Exodus 4:1) Moses is getting a little reckless here. God had just told him that the Israelites would listen to him. The problem is not that Moses won't be believed, but that Moses doesn't want to do what God is telling him to do.

What was God's reply?

> God is very patient. "Okay, you want proof? Here's three miraculous signs for you." (Exodus 4:2-9)

4) Excuse No. 4: "I don't talk so good." (Exodus 4:10) By the way, was Moses' statement true? He might have thought that of himself, but Acts 7:22 says that he was powerful in speech. Even though God provided Aaron as an interpreter, we'll see in later chapters that it was Moses who did a lot of the speaking. He must have had a lot more talent and ability than he admitted to.

What was God's reply?

> a) I made your mouth (Exodus 4:11). I'll see to it that you have the ability to speak.
>
> b) Not only will I help you speak, I'll teach you what to say (Exodus 4:12).

5) Excuse No. 5: "I don't want to do it. Pick somebody else." (Exodus 4:13)

What was God's response?

> a) God got mad (Exodus 4:14). By this time it was obvious that the problem was not one of ability – particularly since God specifically told Moses that He would give him the skills and abilities needed for the task and that the people would listen. The problem was one of the heart. Moses just didn't want to obey God's call.
>
> b) Even so, God was willing to meet every objection. "You don't want to do it? Alright, Aaron will be your assistant." (Exodus 4:14-17)

Lesson: When God calls us to do something, He also gives us the ability to do it. Excuses don't cut it. Though God is amazingly patient, He still requires obedience. The question is not whether God's plan will be accomplished – it will be, but whether we will have a part in that plan.

IV.   Practicing What You Preach (Exodus 4:18-26)

Though Moses reluctantly obeyed God's command to go back to Egypt in order to rescue the Israelites, his heart wasn't in it. It's ironic that the man chosen to rescue God's covenant people was, himself, not obedient to the covenant. He hadn't circumcised his son as God had instructed. If Moses' wife had not intervened, God would have killed Moses for this neglect.

Lesson: Our actions need to conform to what we say we believe. A lot of people seem to think that if they've been called by God, it gives them a license to live however they like. God's standards are for everybody else, but don't apply to them. This isn't true. God doesn't make exceptions for leaders. If anything, leaders should be all the more careful that they live what they preach.

It's interesting that in this passage, God calls Israel His firstborn son (Exodus 4:22). In other words, God has brought the Israelite people into a family relationship with Himself. You don't mess with God's kids! Because the Egyptians won't let the people go, God says that He will kill the firstborn of Egypt.

Lesson: As Christians we should take comfort from this. We also are called God's children. We are in God's household or family. As God's children we can be sure that God will take a very dim view of anyone who messes with us!

V.   Warm Welcome (Exodus 4:27-31)

Most of the time our fears aren't justified. When we are doing God's will, He not only gives us the strength to do it, He also prepares the way. Moses was afraid that he wouldn't be accepted by his people. When they saw the evidence that He was sent by God, and that God cared about their situation, the elders of the people bowed down and worshiped.

Lesson: Don't let your fears prevent you from doing what God asks of you. It is not our job to determine results. It's our job to obey. God will take care of the results. He will fulfill what He has promised.

ೞ೦౪

Let My People Go!
(Exodus 5:1-10:29)

Introduction: We're not told how long the Egyptians enslaved the Israelites. It was probably at least a hundred years by the time God chose Moses to deliver them. Why so long? One major reason is that the people weren't ready to be rescued. Moses tried to do it, in his own strength, when he was about 40 years old. The people rejected him as leader.

You can't free somebody against their will. It wasn't until the people were ready for change that God could do something for them. It wasn't until the Israelites turned to God and cried out to Him, that He sent a deliverer.

I.   Sometimes It Gets Worse Before It Gets Better (Exodus 5:1-21)

Things don't always work out the way we hope. Even though we cry out to God; even though He cares for us, the answer to our prayers and cries may be a long time coming. Sometimes, God's answer to our prayers even seems to make things worse.

Moses and Aaron went to Pharaoh and delivered God's message to let the people go. Far from agreeing to the request, Pharaoh made conditions worse than they already were. The work quotas were kept the same, but raw materials were withheld. There were three results. First, inferior product was turned out. Secondly, production fell off. Thirdly, the Egyptians blamed the workers.

Tangent: If you are ever in the position where you have people working under you, it is your responsibility to see that they have whatever is needed in order to do the work. Unreasonable demands not only undermine worker loyalty, but will result in inferior product. Don't blame the workers for low output if you haven't produced an environment and given them the tools that make it possible to do the work. Beating up on the workers won't cure production problems.

The Israelite elders greeted Moses with joy when he arrived with the message that God had sent him to deliver them from slavery. But, when the request to let the people go resulted in even greater hardship, they turned on Moses and blamed him for their difficulties.

Lesson: Just because you are God's person doesn't make you immune from criticism. (How many of you have ever criticized your boss at work or your church leaders?) The messenger will often be blamed for the message. The test of a leader is how he reacts to the criticism and blame. Does he throw in the towel? Does he make counter-accusations? Or, does he go forward with the task God has given him? Moses hadn't wanted the task God thrust on him. Yet it is significant that when his request to Pharaoh back-fired and the people turned on him, he didn't give up. Instead he turned to God.

II.   Tough Times Don't Cancel God's Promises (Exodus 5:22-6:11)

Why do you think that God sometimes allows things to get worse?

> Just because times are tough doesn't mean that God has abandoned you. Though the Israelites couldn't see it just yet, God was preparing to demonstrate His power in an unforgettable way.

God's response to Moses is interesting. God didn't apologize. In essence, He said, "The situation is under control. I've got Pharaoh just where I want him. Now that you have exhausted all your options, I can work." God then, proceeded to repeat the promises He had already made about delivering the people from bondage.

Lesson: There are several things we can learn from this:

> 1) Don't be discouraged when you follow God's leading and things seem to go wrong. The story isn't over.

> 2) God is faithful. He will fulfill the promises He has made even though we can't see how.

> 3) God will often allow situations to go bad so that there can be no question that deliverance is from Him, and not a result of human cleverness or effort.

We have a saying, "Once burned, twice shy." When Moses went back to the elders and told them what God said, they weren't willing to listen. They were discouraged because of the way things had turned out. It is when we are discouraged that we especially need to listen to God instead of turning away from Him.

III.   The Great Contest

The stage is now set for one of the most dramatic confrontations in history. On one side is Pharaoh who does not recognize God and is oppressing God's people. On the other side is Moses who represents God's people. But they are discouraged and are fearful that Moses' interference will bring even more trouble down on their heads.

Why the plagues?

> On a much more significant level, however, the contest is between God and the gods of Egypt. Through 10 plagues which He brings down on Egypt, God demonstrates His superiority over their gods. The plagues, especially the first and last ones, showed the impotence of the Egyptian deities. In Exodus 12:12, God says, "On that same night I will pass through Egypt and strike down every firstborn – both men and animals – and I will bring judgment on all the gods of Egypt. I am the LORD." (NIV) The purpose of the plagues is repeated in Numbers 33:3-4, "The Israelites set out from Rameses on the fifteenth day of the first month, the day after the Passover. They marched out boldly in full view of all the Egyptians, who were burying all their firstborn, whom the LORD had struck down among them; for the LORD had brought judgment on their gods." (NIV)

> A.   Copycat Miracles (Exodus 7:8-8:15)

> Pharaoh first demanded that Moses perform a miracle to prove his authority to deliver a message from God. At God's direction, Moses had Aaron throw his rod down. It became a snake just as Moses' rod had at the burning bush. There was just one problem. Pharaoh's magicians could do the same

thing. Even though Aaron's rod ate the others, Pharaoh wasn't impressed and refused to listen.

As a result, God began a series of plagues. The first was to turn the water of the Nile River into blood. This was a judgment on two of the Egyptian gods. The first is Hapi, the god of the Nile. The other is Orisis who supposedly caused the Nile to flood every year. The floods brought new topsoil into the fields from upstream – thus rejuvenating the croplands. Now, instead of re-vitalizing the land, the Nile became a source of pollution and death.

The next plague, was swarms of frogs. This was against the goddess Hekt who was supposed to help bring life into the world. She was thought to help during childbirth. Now, her symbol the frog, brought death instead of life.

But the magicians were able to duplicate the miracles again, so Pharaoh remained unyielding. (By the way, it's worth noting that while the magicians were able to duplicate the plagues, they weren't able to stop them!)

Application: These incidents raise a couple of interesting points:

> 1) Not all miracles are from God.
>
> 2) It can be hard to tell the difference between the two.
>
> We have the same problem today. There are many people who claim to perform miracles. Some are counterfeit. In speaking of the coming of the "man of lawlessness" Paul writes, "The coming of the lawless one will be in accordance with the work of Satan displayed in all kinds of counterfeit miracles, signs and wonders, and in every sort of evil that deceives those who are perishing. They perish because they refused to love the truth and so be saved." (2 Thessalonians 2:9-10 NIV)

On the other hand, some miracles may even be genuine. In regard to the judgment Jesus said, "Many will say to me on that day, 'Lord, Lord, did we not prophesy in your name, and in your name drive out demons and perform many miracles?' Then I will tell them plainly, 'I never knew you. Away from me, you evildoers!'" (Matthew 7:22-23 NIV) Jesus doesn't deny that they performed miracles. He doesn't argue that they were frauds. They are condemned, not because they made false claims but, because they did evil.

So, how can we tell which miracles are genuine? How can we tell who is approved by God, and who is not? It may be very difficult to tell. I suggest three tests:

> 1) Does the message the miracle is supposed to validate agree with what is taught in Scripture? If not, then it is either counterfeit, or is not from God.
>
> 2) What is the purpose? Does the miracle honor God? Does it give glory to Christ? If the intent of a miracle is to build up or enhance the reputation of the miracle-worker, it's not from God.
>
> 3) Check out the life-style of the ones doing the miracle. Do their lives show the fruit of the Spirit? If not, you can be sure that the spirit by which they perform miracles is not from God.

B.   The Finger Of God (Exodus 8:16-19)

Pharaoh remained unimpressed by the first two plagues. His magicians were able to duplicate them. As far as Pharaoh was concerned, there was nothing in them which proved that Moses, and his God were any greater than the gods of Egypt. So, God raised the intensity level. The magicians couldn't touch the next plague of gnats. This caused them to acknowledge that God was at work (Exodus 8:19).

In spite of his magicians' recognition of God's work, Pharaoh would not listen. Why wouldn't he listen?

> He hardened his heart. The same thing is true of many people today. They refuse to acknowledge God. The problem is not evidence. There is plenty of evidence around for God's existence. The reason more people don't acknowledge Him and His authority is hardness of heart. They deny God to excuse their own evil lifestyles. Listening to God involves the denial of self. As long as our hearts are filled with self, there is no room in our hearts for God.

C.   God Makes A Distinction (Exodus 8:20-10:29)

Up till now the plagues had affected everyone equally. A lot of people ask what is the point of serving God, if they have to go through the same things as everybody else. That's really the wrong question, as we ought to be serving God out of love for Him, not what we can get out of the relationship.

Even so, it's better to serve God from a poor motive than not to serve Him at all. And, there certainly are benefits to belonging to God. Not the least of them is the hope of eternal life. But even here on earth, those who serve God receive blessings that others don't.

Starting with the fourth plague, flies, God began to show the Egyptians that there was a difference between them and His people. The Israelites were spared the remainder of the plagues while the Egyptians suffered.

After the flies, came a plague on livestock. This was another real blow to the gods of the Egyptians. The cow goddess, Hathor, was one of the main deities. We'll see that when the Israelites turned to idolatry at Mt. Sinai, this is the goddess they copied.

After the plague on cattle came boils, hail, locusts and darkness. The darkness, again, was a special blow against the Egyptian gods. They worshiped a whole bunch of gods connected with light and the sun. Aten was the disk of the sun. Atum-Re, was supposed to give life to the Pharaohs. (The Pharaohs were considered divine because their life derived from the sun.) Horus, the 'sun of the horizon' was one of the principle Egyptian gods. Mahes represented the destructive heat of the sun.

None of these plagues were sufficient to break Pharaoh's will. Even though his country was being destroyed, he still refused to obey. Thus, he set himself up for the most serious plague of all – the death of the firstborn.

IV.   Downward Spiral

It's interesting to watch the progression of Pharaoh's responses to what Moses requests during the plagues.

	Moses' Request	Pharaoh's Response
1st (5:1)	festival in desert	increased work load (5:9)
2nd (7:16)	worship in desert	heart became hard (7:22)
3rd (8:1)	worship	offer sacrifices (8:8) hardened his heart (8:15)
4th (8:20)	worship	sacrifice here (8:25)
5th (8:27)	three day journey	don't go far (8:28) hardened his heart (8:32)
6th (9:1)	worship	heart unyielding (9:7)
7th (9:13)	worship	sinned, hardened his heart (9:34)
8th (10:3)	worship	Lord hardened his heart (10:20)
9th		leave flocks, herds (10:24) Lord hardened (10:27)

Moses requested permission for the Israelites to leave at least 8 different times. On at least 5 of these occasions, Pharaoh hardened his heart. Though he seemed to be giving in a little more, as the plagues progressed, the truth is that as soon as he got relief from the plague of the moment, he changed his mind, went back on his promise and refused to let the people go. It's important to note that the last two times, it says that God hardened Pharaoh's heart.

Lesson: God will help us along whatever path we choose. If we choose to serve Him, He will work in us and change us so we become more like Him. If we persist in hardening our hearts, He'll help us do that, too. Choose wisely!

ଽଠେଔ

With a Mighty Hand
(Exodus 11:1-13:16)

Introduction: In spite of increasingly severe pressure, Pharaoh continued to refuse to let the Israelites go from Egypt. At the end of the 9th plague, Pharaoh told Moses to never appear before him again or he would be executed. In the face of such constant and firm refusal, God prepared one final blow which was so devastating that the Egyptians not only let the people go, they urged them to go.

I.   Fair Warning (Exodus 11:1-8)

One of God's characteristics is love. He does not take pleasure in the death of anyone, not even the wicked (Ezekiel 18:32). Even when God must punish, He gives warning. Before the flood, He gave mankind 120 years to shape up. He gave Sodom and Gomorrah warning. He gave the Canaanites 400 years. Now He gives Pharaoh, and all Egypt, a final warning. Even though Pharaoh has told him to get lost, Moses does not leave until he tells Pharaoh what God is going to do.

Though Moses has conveyed God's warning, it's interesting that one of his own besetting problems makes another appearance while doing it. Pharaoh has reacted to the request to let the Israelites go with anger. Moses meets anger with anger. Is this one of the factors which feeds Pharaoh's stubbornness? There is no indication in the text that this is the case – Pharaoh was plenty stubborn without any provocation – but it can happen. James 1:19-20 says, "My dear brothers, take note of this: Everyone should be quick to listen, slow to speak and slow to become angry, for man's anger does not bring about the righteous life that God desires." (NIV) We need to be careful that even when we have plenty of reason to become angry, that our anger does not hinder someone from responding to God as he should.

II.   So That My Wonders May Be Multiplied (Exodus 11:9-10)

You would think that the Egyptians would have learned the lesson from seeing the previous 9 plagues take place just as Moses had warned. But there are two things which kept them from doing so.

> 1) The text states that the Lord hardened Pharaoh's heart. Pharaoh had hardened his own heart often enough. Now God is going to confirm the direction Pharaoh has already chosen. If we continually refuse to yield to God's will, the time comes when He says, "Your will be done."

> 2) God hardened Pharaoh's heart so that His (God's) wonders would be multiplied in Egypt. God wanted there to be no doubt that the deliverance of the Israelites from bondage was not the result of human effort, but was from God. He also used the last plague as a decisive blow against the religion of Egypt. In Egyptian mythology, Pharaoh, himself was divine. It was the duty of the first-born to make prayers and offerings to him in the afterlife. But with the heir dead, those prayers and offerings could not be made. Similarly, a duty of the firstborn of all Egyptians was to keep the memory of his ancestors alive. The death of the firstborn destroyed the whole system. It proved God's claim that the firstborn belong to Him.

III.   When I See The Blood (Exodus 12:1-13)

In most of the earlier plagues, God had made a distinction between the Israelites and the Egyptians. The plagues affected only the parts of the land where the Egyptians lived, but not the district of Goshen where the Israelites lived. Now, God is going to make the distinction even more obvious. The difference will not be based on geography, but on obedience.

God tells His people to make a sacrifice. It's interesting that before sending the prior plagues, Moses had asked for permission to go three days away so the sacrifices the Israelites were to make would not offend the Egyptians (Exodus 8:26). Now, they are to make sacrifices right where they are, regardless of what the Egyptians think.

Lesson: We should try not to be offensive to others of different beliefs and religions. There comes a time, however, when we have to choose to do what God asks of us even if it offends. The Egyptians had refused to allow the people to go away and sacrifice, so the sacrificing was done right in front of them.

God gave specific instructions about the sacrifice:

> 1) He chose what the sacrifice was to be. God did not allow the people to sacrifice any animal they happened to fancy. It had to be a lamb or kid.
>
> 2) It had to be a year-old male.
>
> 3) It had to be without defect.
>
> 4) It had to be sufficient for the number of people in the household.
>
> 5) It had to be eaten indoors. (See Exodus 12:22.)
>
> 6) It had to be eaten with unleavened bread and bitter herbs.
>
> 7) The people had to be ready for action.
>
> 8) Most importantly, they had to put some of the blood of the sacrifice on the tops and sides of the doorway to their house.

God told the people, explicitly, that He was going to pass through Egypt to strike down the firstborn in every household. Only those households which had the blood on the doorways would be exempted. It was the blood which stood between them and death.

IV.   A Lasting Ordinance (Exodus 12:14-20)

The Passover is one of the most momentous events in Jewish history. It was so pivotal that God commanded them to reckon the beginning of their calendar year from it (Exodus 12:2). They were also to celebrate the Passover every year.

V.   Passed Over (Exodus 12:21-42)

Upon receiving the instructions, the Israelites did two very significant things:

    1) They bowed down and worshiped (Exodus 12:27).

    2) Then, they obeyed (12:28).

Application: It's incredibly important for us to follow their example. Obedience without worship is really just going through motions. On the other hand, to worship without doing demonstrates a dead faith. Jesus said, "Why do you call me, 'Lord, Lord,' and do not do what I say?" (Luke 6:46 NIV) James writes, "As the body without the spirit is dead, so faith without deeds is dead." (James 2:26 NIV)

If the Israelites had not obeyed what God had told them to do, they would have suffered the same fate as the Egyptians. Presumably, if any Egyptians had had enough faith to follow the instructions, they would have been spared.

At midnight, the plague struck just as God said it would. Not a single household was spared – regardless of social or economic position. In this one thing at least, all the Egyptians were totally equal. It's the same today. We all will face the consequences of disobedience, no matter who we are. If we are not under the protection of Christ's blood, we will perish.

In spite of what Pharaoh had told Moses at the end of the ninth plague, he summoned him and Aaron and finally gave permission for the Israelites to leave Egypt. Not just Pharaoh, but all the Egyptians wanted them to leave. The fear was that their remaining in the land would cause even more death (Exodus 12:33).

Not only did the Egyptians urge the Israelites to leave, they were willing to give them anything they asked for. "Take anything you want. Just go!" No doubt the Israelites considered this compensation for all the years of hardship they had endured.

There's another important thing which is mentioned, almost in passing. Exodus 12:38 says that it wasn't just the Israelites who left

Egypt, but a large number of other people went with them. It is this crowd of non-Israelite people who became a source of real spiritual trouble later on. The text does not say so, but I wonder if this isn't the reason for the instruction which is emphasized in the next section.

VI.   No Foreigner (Exodus 12:43-51)

The story of the Exodus is interrupted by another block of instructions. First, God emphasizes that the Passover celebration is only for those who are in covenant relationship with God. Foreigners are not to take part. If an alien does want to celebrate it, he must first submit to circumcision. In other words, he must place himself into covenant relationship with God before he can partake of the Passover.

Application: Today, we as Christians celebrate our deliverance from sin by partaking of the Lord's Supper or Communion. It is not for those who are outside of Christ. In the book of Hebrews it says, "We have an altar from which those who minister at the tabernacle have no right to eat." (Hebrews 13:10 NIV) On the basis of this, some churches have a policy of not allowing anyone except members partake of Communion. My personal opinion is that it is best to allow each individual to determine whether he takes it or not. Paul writes, "A man ought to examine himself before he eats of the bread and drinks of the cup." (1 Corinthians 11:28 NIV) But, there is no doubt that those who are not in Christ should not take Communion. Paul goes on to say that those who take it in an unworthy manner bring judgment on themselves.

VII.   What Does This Mean? (Exodus 13:1-16)

In the first part of chapter 13, God stresses the importance of passing on, not only the celebration of the Passover to following generations but, the meaning of it. One of the lessons of the Passover is that all the firstborn belong to God. Secondly, it takes a sacrifice to redeem.

There are a lot of parallels between Passover and the sacrifice which was made to redeem us from sin. Here are some of them:

1) God chose what the sacrifice was to be.

Parallel: We are not capable of saving ourselves. God is the One who provided the sacrifice for us.

2) The sacrifice had to be a lamb or kid.

Parallel: Jesus is called the 'Lamb of God' (John 1:29).

3) The sacrifice had to be without defect.

Parallel: Jesus was without sin (Hebrews 4:15).

4) The lamb had to be sufficient for the number of people in the household.

Parallel: Jesus' sacrifice is sufficient for the entire world (1 John 2:2).

5) The Passover meal had to be eaten indoors.

Parallel: Only those within God's household (the church) have the right to eat the emblems of Christ's sacrifice.

6) The Passover lamb had to be eaten with unleavened bread and bitter herbs.

Parallel: Leaven represents sin. If we have not been cleansed from sin, we have no right to eat of the emblems. (See Hebrews 10:22.) Just as the Israelites were to get rid of all leaven before the Passover, those who are in Christ are to live holy and pure lives (1 Peter 1:15-16).

7) The people had to be ready for action.

Parallel: Christians also are to be prepared for action (1 Peter 1:13-19).

8) Most importantly, the Israelites had to put some of the blood of the sacrifice on the tops and sides of the doorway.

Parallel: It is the blood of Christ which covers our sin and shields us from God's wrath (Romans 5:9). It is through Christ's blood that we are brought within God's household (Ephesians 2:13-22).

ಬಂಡ

Crossing the Sea
(Exodus 13:17-15:21)

Introduction: The plagues are done. Egypt lies ruined. There is at least one dead in every house. Pharaoh and all the people beg the Israelites to leave. They shower the Israelites with wealth as an added incentive to leave. But the Israelites have another major hurdle to cross before they exit Egypt. Though they have seen ample evidence of God's power, their faith will be tested to the limit before they see salvation.

I.   God Will Not Let You Be Tempted Beyond What You Can Bear (Exodus 13:17-18)

Sometimes our biggest tests come, not when things are bleak but, when things are going really well. After the Passover, the Israelites must have been on an emotional high. They saw their oppressors ruined. They not only acquired gold, silver and clothing (see Exodus 12:35-36), they must have also acquired weapons. Exodus 13:18 says that they left Egypt armed for battle. In light of the experiences they had just witnessed and come through, the Israelites probably thought they they were ready to take on the world. But God knew better. He knew that even though they were armed, they were not ready to face war. Because of this, God led them toward the promised land, the long way around.

Lesson: 1ˢᵗ Corinthians 10:13 says, "…God is faithful; he will not let you be tempted beyond what you can bear. But when you are tempted, he will also provide a way out so that you can stand up under it." (NIV) We can be sure that God allows us to be in whatever situation we're in because He has also given us the strength to handle it. He will never allow us to face something that is beyond what we can cope with.

II.   Keeping Promises (Exodus 13:19)

God kept His promise to deliver the Israelites from Egypt. But there was another promise which needed to be kept as well. Joseph had made his brothers swear that when the time of deliverance came, they would take his bones out of Egypt with them (Genesis 50:25). Although almost 400 years have passed, Moses fulfills the oath by doing what Joseph asked.

Lesson: We need to keep our promises no matter how much time has passed. Time does not erase the vows we have made.

III.   Guidance (Exodus 13:20-22)

God doesn't tell us to do something and, then, leave us without direction. In the case of the Israelites, there could be no question about which direction God wanted them to take. He guided them by pillars of cloud and fire.

Question: How does God guide His people today? There are two main ways:

> 1) Through His word. "Your word is a lamp to my feet and a light for my path." (Psalm 119:105 NIV)
>
> 2) By his Spirit. "But when he, the Spirit of truth, comes, he will guide you into all truth. He will not speak on his own; he will speak only what he hears, and he will tell you what is yet to come." (John 16:13 NIV) "I keep asking that the God of our Lord Jesus Christ, the glorious Father, may give you the Spirit of wisdom and revelation, so that you may know him better." (Ephesians 1:17 NIV)

IV.   A Lesson Unlearned (Exodus 14:1-9)

Even though the Egyptians had seen, and suffered, the plagues they quickly forgot God's power. The display of God's power did not motivate them either to seek Him or to repent. Once again, God helped them along the path they had already chosen. He hardened their hearts. The reason? So that the Egyptians would recognize Him as the Lord through the disaster which was going to occur, and for God to gain glory.

Lesson: God will be glorified. The question is how? Will we freely give Him the glory which is His due, or will He receive it through the disaster we bring on ourselves from not giving God His due? It's our choice.

It's interesting that the decision that the Egyptians made to pursue the Israelites apparently was not motivated by the idea of taking revenge for all the disasters Egypt had suffered. Instead, it was an economic decision. They were worried about what they would do without the services of the Israelites (Exodus 14:5). Soon, they wouldn't have to worry about it at all.

It's also interesting that the decision to pursue wasn't just Pharaoh's. His officials were in agreement with it.

Any way you look at it, the Egyptians mounted a major military expedition to try to bring the Israelites back. Our popular image of the pursuit is of chariots. Six hundred of the best chariots are specifically mentioned (Exodus 14:7). In addition, there were chariots of lessor quality. But, the text also indicates that cavalry and infantry were involved (Exodus 14:9). In order to supply the army, and especially fodder for the horses, there must have been a whole horde of camp followers as well. We don't know the total number of men involved, but it must have been several thousand.

V.   Be Still (Exodus 14:10-14)

Exodus 14:10 presents quite a contrast to the picture of Exodus14:8 where the Israelites are described as marching out boldly. When they see the Egyptian pursuit, the Israelites are terrified. In one moment, they move from joy and exultation over their deliverance, to despair and panic. It's so easy to forget God's promises and what He has done in the past! This is one reason why we need to continually remind ourselves. This is why it is important to keep reading and studying the Scriptures so that we don't forget.

Moses told them to be still. This is good advice when we are in a panic over what is going on. We need to remember that no matter what is happening, God is still in control. "Be still, and know that I am God; I will be exalted among the nations, I will be exalted in the earth." (Psalm 46:10 NIV)

VI.   Move On (Exodus 14:15-18)

Though Moses told the people to be still, God told them to move on.

Lesson: There's an important lesson here. Being calm is not the same as being passive. Relying on God does not mean taking no action. In reality, relying on God involves obeying what He's said to do. In this case, God told the people He would deliver them. He told them to move. Even though the barriers looked impossible, the people needed to step out in faith believing that God would keep His promise even though it looked impossible from a human point of view.

VII.   Crossing On Dry Ground (Exodus 14:19-22)

God not only told the Israelites to move, He put a barrier between them and the Egyptians. The cloud moved between the two groups. It's interesting that the very same thing, the pillar of cloud, had very different effects on each group. To the Egyptians, it brought darkness, to the Israelites it brought light.

Application: The same sort of thing happens today. Paul likened his ministry to a smell. To those being saved, it was the fragrance of life. But to the unsaved, it was the smell of death (2 Corinthians 2:14-16). It is not the message or the thing itself which changes, but our response to it which determines whether we are saved or condemned.

Because of their obedience to God's instructions, not only were the Israelites given light, a way of escape opened up for them where there was no way. It's important to note, however, that it took courage and faith to take advantage of that way. It must have been frightening to walk between those walls of water. Yet, they did it. It was the only way. If they had been unwilling to take it, they would have perished.

VIII.   Difficult Driving (Exodus 14:23-28)

The Egyptians tried to follow. Yet their attempt to do exactly the same thing as the Israelites ended in disaster.

1) The Lord threw them into confusion (Exodus 14:24).

2) The chariots bogged down – either because the ground couldn't support the wheels, or the wheels came off (Exodus 14:25).

3) The sea came back into its place and drowned them all (Exodus 14:28).

Application: Two groups of people try to do the same thing. One group lives, the other dies. What makes the difference? The Israelites were trying to do God's will, the Egyptians were trying to thwart it. Why do we do the things we do? Are we being obedient, or are we following our own desires? Whether we follow God's will, will determine the outcome of our actions.

IX.   Fearing The Lord (Exodus 14:29-31)

The crossing of the sea and the destruction of the Egyptian army impressed the Israelites even more than all of the plagues they had witnessed. The text says that it was after this that they not only feared the Lord, but put their trust in Him.

What does it mean to fear the Lord? There are probably several things involved, but I suggest that one of them is a reverent awe. It not only recognizes God's power, but it causes us to give God His due. It moves us to worship.

X.   A Song For The Lord (Exodus 15:1-21)

After crossing the sea, the Israelites composed and sang a song to God. A lot could be said about it but I'll just mention a couple things.

1) The crossing caused the Israelites to recognize the attributes of God. Exodus 15:11 mentions His holiness and His glory.

2) They recognized the effect of the crossing on other peoples. After this, there could be no doubt about God's superiority over the pagan gods. There could be no doubt that the Israelites were God's people.

Question: Can the people around us see God working in our lives and situation?

XI.   A Metaphor Of Salvation

There are a lot of parallels between the crossing of the sea and the salvation which God gives us through Christ.

> 1) Just as it took faith for the Israelites to cross the sea, salvation from sin requires faith as well (Romans 10:9-10).
>
> 2) Both involve obedience (Mark 16:16).
>
> 3) 1st Corinthians 10:1-2 equates the crossing to baptism. Without the crossing, the Israelites could not have been delivered from Egypt. Without baptism we cannot be delivered from sin.
>
> 4) Christ is the agent in both. 1st Corinthians 10:4 specifically states that Christ was with the Israelites. We are baptized into Christ's death in order to rise to walk in a new life (Romans 6:3-5).
>
> 5) Just like there was no way out of Egypt, there is no way out of the consequences of our sin. Just as God redeemed the Israelites (Exodus 15:13), He redeems us from sin. If we do not accept the way out which God provides, the result is destruction. Will we take the way He's provided, or not?

 හ○ශ

Trusting Daily
(Exodus 15:22-18:27)

Introduction: It's natural to turn to God when we are caught up in situations which are clearly bigger than we are and beyond our ability to control. It is said that there are no atheists in foxholes. What is not so easy, however, is to trust God and rely on Him to supply our needs in the normal course of every-day life. All too often we tend to forget God when things are going well. If all is as we think it should be, we tend to think that it's that way because of our own goodness or efforts. On the other hand, when things start to go wrong, we tend to blame it on God. We start to doubt His goodness and His promises to provide and care for us. We begin to question whether we wouldn't have been better off not following God at all.

The miraculous crossing of the Red Sea and the destruction of the Egyptian army impressed the Israelites more than all the plagues they had witnessed in Egypt. Exodus 14:31 says that after experiencing the crossing the Israelites put their trust in God. After the spiritual high of being delivered and singing God's praise for their deliverance, the Israelites found that they still had to go on with daily life. They came face to face with another set of challenges which would test their trust.

I.   From Bitter To Sweet (Exodus 15:22-27)

The first challenge the Israelites faced after leaving Egypt had to do with one of life's basic necessities – water. For three days they didn't find any. Then, when they did, it wasn't fit to drink.

You can tell a lot about someone's character by how they first respond to difficulties. What was the Israelites' reaction to the water situation?

> They grumbled. Even though they had witnessed God's power and had just experienced a miraculous deliverance from Egyptian slavery, they still grumbled. Though they had

put their trust in God, they apparently didn't believe that God would provide what they needed.

Question: Are we the kind of people who grumble instead of trusting God to supply our needs?

God showed Moses how to make the water drinkable. But this raises another question: Why didn't God just supply sweet water to begin with?

Exodus 15:25 says that God tested the people.

What does that mean?

Surely God did not test them in the sense of needing to find out what kind of people they were. God already knows what we are. Also, God did not test them in the sense of putting them into temptation. James 1:13 assures us that God does not tempt people. So in what way, or for what purpose does God test us? I think there are two aspects to testing.

1) God puts us into difficult situations so that we can discover and recognize what sort of people we are.

2) God tests in the sense of refining us. Hardship and trouble temper and mature us. They cause us to rely more fully upon God rather than ourselves. They give us the opportunity to increase our faith.

Along with the testing, God gave a promise. He told the Israelites that if they obeyed; if they were willing to follow His leading, then they would not be afflicted with any of the diseases which were prevalent among the Egyptians. There isn't always a direct connection between sin and disease. But it is interesting how many diseases are contracted through sin (such as sexually transmitted diseases and addictions) and/or made worse by living a lifestyle which is at odds with biblical principles (such as over-eating).

II.   Meat And Bread (Exodus 16:1-36)

The next challenge was lack of food. About 45 days after the crossing of the Red Sea the food they had brought from Egypt ran out. What was their reaction?

1) They grumbled.

2) They distorted facts. They selectively recalled the good things they had in Egypt. They conveniently forgot or ignored the oppression they had been under. They forgot that they themselves had called out to God for relief (Exodus 2:23). They forgot that the reason they were in the desert to begin with was that God had heard them and rescued them (Exodus 3:9-10).

3) They forgot God's promises. Clear back in Genesis 15:16 God had promised Abraham that the Israelites would return to Palestine after their stay in Egypt. God had also told Moses, in Exodus 3:12, that the people would worship Him at Mt. Sinai. It doesn't take a genius to figure out that if they were going to worship at Mt. Sinai and return to Palestine, that God would not let them starve to death before they got there.

Application: What are some of God's promises we forget?

a) Obey your parents that it may go well with you and you will enjoy long life (Ephesians 6:1-3).

b) I have a place for you (John 14:2-3).

c) I will never forsake you (Hebrews 13:5).

4) They questioned motives. They accused Moses and Aaron of leading them out to the desert to starve. First, who was it that was leading them? It was God, Himself. Remember that Lord led them with a pillar of cloud by day and a pillar of fire by night (Exodus 13:21-22). It wasn't Moses who brought the people into the desert, it was God. Secondly, what was God's purpose for choosing the route He did? God didn't send them to Palestine by the short route in order to spare

them from warfare – for which they were not ready (Exodus 13:17-18). God led them into the desert to spare them from something far worse than a little hunger. Also, were they really in danger of starving? Hardly! Don't forget that they had large herds of cattle and other livestock with them. Sure, it would have been an economic hardship to butcher some of their flocks and herds, but there was enough meat to last them a long time.

Lesson: Before we grumble at some hardship we're facing, we need to stop and think. Is it possible that God is sparing us from something far worse? Can we learn to look at the difficulties we face as blessings? "And we know that in all things God works for the good of those who love him, who have been called according to his purpose." (Romans 8:28 NIV)

God had a greater purpose in this situation than merely sparing the people from combat. God promised that He would provide food, but there was a catch. The food was to be gathered in a certain way. They were to gather only enough for one day at a time, except on the sixth day when they were to gather enough for two days.

What was the purpose for providing food in this way?

1) Exodus 16:4 says that God used this as a test. He wanted to see whether the people would follow instructions. He was trying to instill a mindset of obedience in them. This was important because a few days later, when they reached Mt. Sinai, God was going to make a covenant with them and give them what we call the Law of Moses. The basic premise of the Law of Moses is: "Keep my decrees and laws, for the man who obeys them will live by them. I am the LORD." (Leviticus 18:5 NIV. See also Romans 10:5.)

How well did the people do in keeping the instructions about gathering manna?

Not too well. Some tried to keep more than they needed for the day (Exodus 16:20). Others went out to gather manna on the Sabbath even though they had been expressly told not to do it (Exodus 16:27). In both cases, the consequences were exactly what they had been warned about.

Lesson: All too often we don't take God at His word. We think we know better. All too often we think that we'll be the exception. But it isn't so. We will always pay a price for disobedience. We would save ourselves a lot of grief if we would just do what God says. We don't have to try everything for ourselves. When someone tells us that we'll burn our finger by sticking it in a flame, we don't have to try it to see whether it's true. In the same way, we don't have to sin in order to find out whether the consequences really are what God says they will be. We need to learn to trust God. Since we've already seen, in our own lives, that certain of God's principles and promises are true, we can rest assured that those we have not personally experienced are also true. We also need to learn from the examples and experiences of others.

> 2) There was a deeper purpose to letting the people experience hunger and then feeding them with manna. Later, in reminding the people about this incident Moses said: "Remember how the LORD your God led you all the way in the desert these forty years, to humble you and to test you in order to know what was in your heart, whether or not you would keep his commands. He humbled you, causing you to hunger and then feeding you with manna, which neither you nor your fathers had known, to teach you that man does not live on bread alone but on every word that comes from the mouth of the LORD." (Deuteronomy 8:2-3 NIV)

> In other words, God was trying to teach them that there are more important things than food. Ultimately it is God's Word which sustains us, not material things. Jesus said, "What good is it for a man to gain the whole world, yet forfeit his soul?" (Mark 8:36 NIV) It is significant that Jesus, Himself, quoted this passage from Deuteronomy to overcome temptation when He was hungry and the devil told him to turn stones into bread (Matthew 4:1-4, Luke 4:1-4).

Application: There are two more things worth noting in regard to the manna.

1) After the feeding of the 5,000, the people asked Jesus for a sign so they could believe on Him (John 6:30-31). As if He had not just given them one! The sign they wanted was to be fed bread from heaven as the Israelites had been fed manna in the wilderness. In response to their demand, Jesus preached an expository sermon on Psalm 78:24 which refers to this incident. In His sermon Jesus told the people that it is He who is the true bread from heaven. His words are spirit and life (John 6:63) which sustain all those who assimilate them.

Question: Are we feeding on the true bread from heaven? Or are we trying to digest things which can never give spiritual life?

2) Exodus 16:17-18 says that people gathered different amounts of manna, yet everyone had enough. How did this work out? The text implies that what everyone gathered was measured and then distributed according to need. In 2 Corinthians 8:13-15 the Apostle Paul used this as an example of how Christians ought to share their resources so that the needs of everyone in the Lord are met. Today my surplus can fill your need while tomorrow your surplus can fill my need.

III.   Water In The Desert (Exodus 17:1-7)

The next challenge again had to do with water. Before, at Marah, there had been plenty of water even though it was not drinkable. This time, there was no water at all. Once again, instead of responding with faith that the Lord would supply what was needed as He had already done before, the people grumbled.

There was an even more serious issue. This time the people questioned whether God was among them (Exodus 17:7). This is particularly ironic because verse 1 specifically states that they traveled "from place to place as the LORD commanded." (NIV) To put it another way, the reason they were in this waterless place to begin with, was that God had sent them there.

Lesson: Don't start to doubt God's presence when His leading is clear. If God takes you somewhere you can be sure that He is with you. Don't judge by outward appearances. If God sends you to a place or tells you to do something, He will supply what you need in order to stay there and to do what He's told you to do.

IV.   Not In Our Own Strength (Exodus 17:8-16)

The Israelites also had to deal with an unprovoked attack. While retelling this event in Deuteronomy 25:17-18, Moses said that the Amalekites picked off the stragglers who were worn out from the journey. It was this incident which caused God to promise the complete destruction of the Amalekites. This was fulfilled centuries later. One of God's principles is: "It is mine to avenge; I will repay…" (Deuteronomy 32:35 NIV) He keeps His promises not only to bless but also to avenge.

Question: There are going to be times in your life when you will be unjustly accused or attacked. How will you respond? Will you try to take vengeance on your own, or will you let God take care of it?

In response to the attack Moses directed Joshua to give battle. The interesting thing to note is that the Israelites won only as long as Moses lifted his hands.

Lesson: It's best not to try to defend yourself at all – but when it is necessary and even when we fight in a just cause, we must not take things into our own hands. We must not depend on our own strength and wisdom. We still need God's power. We are dependent upon Him.

V.   Order From Chaos (Exodus 18:1-27)

A different sort of challenge is the problem of leadership and organizational structure. It's very easy to get overwhelmed by the mechanics of just trying to make an organization work. We can become so busy putting out brushfires that it's impossible to get anything done. Structure is necessary if a large group is to function.

Moses' father-in-law provided a wise plan to solve the organizational bottleneck Moses and the Israelites were experiencing. It's important to understand that Jethro offered his plan with a condition: It was only to be implemented if God commanded it (Exodus 18:23). Apparently the plan did have God's approval because it was implemented. Because of the system which Jethro proposed, people's cases were judged quickly and efficiently. Moses only had to deal with the difficult cases which set precedents and/or required a ruling from God.

Lesson: We all need to learn to listen to wise counsel. Don't hesitate to take godly advice from people who love the Lord and have your best interests in mind.

Conclusion: 2 Peter 1:3 says: "His divine power has given us everything we need for life and godliness through our knowledge of him who called us by his own glory and goodness." (NIV) As long as we are living for God, we can rest assured that He will provide everything we need. We don't have to be anxious or frightened when we encounter difficult situations. If we do experience hardship, or lack something, we can be sure that God is using it to teach us a valuable lesson or to increase our faith. The question is how will we respond? Will we trust God to supply what we need, or will we grumble?

ഇൽ

Covenant Codified
(Exodus 19:1 and following)

Introduction: The giving of the Mosaic Law at Mt. Sinai is one of the pivotal events in all history. Through it the children of Israel were transformed from a group of families with a common ancestor into a nation. By it the Israelites were separated from all other peoples. Through it God entered into a covenant relationship with an entire people. Most important of all, it foreshadowed the much greater New Covenant, God would provide through Jesus Christ.

I.   On Eagles' Wings

God had promised to bring the people of Israel to Sinai. Now, in the third month, on the first day of the month, the promise was fulfilled.

How many days did the journey to Sinai take?

> The Passover took place on the 14th day of the first month (Exodus 12:17-18). Assuming a 30-day month, 16 days were left in the first month after they left Egypt. Another 30 days puts them at Sinai, for a total of 46 days en route.

What metaphor does God use to describe how He brought the people to Sinai?

> God said that He carried the people on eagles' wings (Exodus 19:4). What does this mean? The metaphor is explained in Deuteronomy 32:10-11. Speaking of God it says, "In a desert land he found him, in a barren and howling waste. He shielded him and cared for him; he guarded him as the apple of his eye, like an eagle that stirs up its nest and hovers over its young, that spreads its wings to catch them and carries them on its pinions." (NIV)

> Most likely, the text refers to the Palestinian Vulture. Adult vultures teach their young to fly by carrying them on their wings. When the young attempt to fly and fall, the adults catch them on their own wings. What God is saying is that

He was there all along to support the Israelites during their journey.

In addition to sustaining His people, God had another purpose in the journey. There are two verses which say that God used the various difficulties the people faced in order to test them (Exodus 15:25, 16:4). Metaphorically, God not only sustained and carried the people on eagles' wings, but was teaching them to fly.

Question: How do we view difficulties? Do we look at them as evidence that God doesn't love us, or do we look at them as evidence of God's helping us to learn to fly?

II.   A Treasured Possession

God had promised that He would bring the people to Mt. Sinai. But why? What did God intend to do there?

God wanted to make a covenant between Himself and the people of Israel. But this raises another question. As a general rule, we are not familiar with covenants.

What is a covenant?

"A covenant is a binding, unbreakable obligation between two parties, based on unconditional love sealed by blood and sacred oath, that creates a relationship in which each party is bound by specific undertakings on each other's behalf. The parties to the covenant place themselves under the penalty of divine retribution should they later attempt to avoid those undertakings. It is a relationship that can only be broken by death." (Malcolm Smith, *The Power Of The Blood Covenant*, Harrison House, Tulsa, Oklahoma, 2002, p. 12-13)

We are not going to be able to do the topic of covenant justice in this lesson. But there are two aspects of covenant in the above definition to which I want to draw special attention.

1) A covenant is founded on unconditional love. It is a relationship which is not earned. It's a relationship which you enter into by choice because you have decided to love the

other person – whether they are lovely or lovable, or not. The relationship is not based on feeling. Ideally, feelings will come as both parties keep the covenant relationship, but that is not what the relationship is based upon. This is why arranged marriages can be, and are, just as successful as those where people choose their own partners. As long as both partners are committed to the relationship; as long as both regard the covenant as something valuable in itself, the marriage will work regardless of how the marriage came about. Feelings are not what is important. Commitment to the relationship; unconditional love, is.

2) Someone enters into a covenant relationship for the good or benefit of the other party. This is particularly true in the case of a covenant between unequal parties. In other words, the stronger or greater person enters a covenant relationship for the good or benefit of the other person. The idea is to serve rather than to get. This is very different from entering into a contract. When someone enters into a contract the primary concern is his own benefit rather than what is good for the other person.

What benefits did God want to give the Israelites by entering into covenant with them?

Exodus 19:5 states that God would view the Israelites as His treasured possession. To put it another way, the Israelites would belong to God in a way that no other peoples would. They would have a special status because they belonged to God not only because He is the Creator, but because they agreed to become His.

Exodus 19:6 says that they would be a kingdom of priests and a holy nation. A priest is someone who acts as a mediator between man and God. He prays for, and offers sacrifices to God for, someone else. What this indicates is that God intended to use the Israelite people to bring God's grace to the world. God was going to use this nation to bring salvation to the whole of mankind. This is an extension of the promise

> God had made to Abraham, "…all peoples on earth will be blessed through you." (Genesis 12:3 NIV)
>
> To be "holy" means to be set apart or separated. God promised that the Israelites would be different or distinct from all other peoples. They were going to be set apart for God's purposes and use.

What was the people's response to God's offer of a covenant relationship?

> They responded by promising to do everything God said. Notice that this was an act of faith because they did not, as yet, know what God would require of them. Their response was based on what they understood of God's character. In Exodus 19:4, God reminded the people of what they had witnessed of His power and faithfulness in Egypt and the journey to Sinai. God had promised that they would come to Sinai. The promise was fulfilled in spite of what, from a human point of view, seemed like overwhelming odds. If God was able to fulfill that promise, He surely would be able to fulfill the promises of the covenant.
>
> It is worth noting that not only here, but after the people had been given the Law, the people still responded by agreeing to obey what God said (Exodus 24:3, 7).

III.   Meet A Holy God (Exodus 19:9-25)

Even though God had offered to enter into a covenant relationship with the people, there was a problem: How can a sinful people approach God, who is totally good, righteous and true? How can they even hear the terms of the covenant if approaching God means death?

> 1) The people needed a mediator – someone to stand between the people and God. Moses performed this role. He went up the mountain to hear God's words, then he relayed what God said to the people and took their response back to God.

2) The people had to be consecrated or sanctified – that is they had to be set apart for God. There is no use pretending that we can enter into covenant without turning away from those things which would break the covenant relationship. Here, the people had to wash their clothes (Exodus 19:10, 14). In Scripture, the image of dirty or filthy clothes is sometimes used as a metaphor for sin. (For example, see Zechariah 3:3-4, Jude 1:23.) By washing their clothes, the people demonstrated that they were renouncing, or turning away from sin.

 The people were also told to abstain from sexual relations (Exodus 19:15). This is a metaphor for devoting oneself to God. Elsewhere in Scripture, turning away from God is pictured in terms of adultery. (For example, Jeremiah 3:8, Ezekiel 23, James 4:4.)

Even though God told the people to abstain, He was not saying that sex is wrong or that abstaining makes one more holy. On the contrary, God established sex and within marriage it is good and holy. There are times, however, when it is appropriate to abstain so that the physical does not distract from concentrating more fully on the spiritual. (For example, see 1 Corinthians 7:5.)

IV.   The Fine Print

God had offered to enter into a covenant relationship with the Israelites. They had accepted and promised to do everything God would tell them. The mediator was appointed. The people were consecrated. But what would the covenant actually contain? It's interesting to note that the covenant God gave at Mt. Sinai follows the same legal form that was used in vassal treaty documents of that time. It's also interesting that this precise form of the covenant was used only during a certain time period. This is an indication of when the Exodus took place – the second millennium B.C. The parts of the covenant are as follows:

1) Preamble. This is where the person who offers the covenant identifies himself. (Exodus 20:2 "I am the LORD your God…" NIV)

2) Historical review. A short summary of the historical context of the covenant and a reminder of what the proposer of the covenant has done on behalf of those to whom the covenant is offered. (Exodus 20:2, "…who brought you out of Egypt, out of the land of slavery." NIV)

3) The stipulations. These are the terms of the covenant – what the people who are in the covenant must do. The terms include not only the 'Ten Commandments' in Exodus 20:3-17, but the whole of the 'Mosaic Law.' That is, every law from Exodus 20 through Numbers 10, is included.

4) Deposition. A copy of the covenant was to be preserved and periodically read to the people so that they would remember the provisions. (Exodus 25:16, "Then put in the ark the Testimony, which I will give you." (NIV), "At the end of every seven years, in the year for canceling debts, during the Feast of Tabernacles, when all Israel comes to appear before the LORD your God at the place he will choose, you shall read this law before them in their hearing. Assemble the people – men, women and children, and the aliens living in your towns – so they can listen and learn to fear the LORD your God and follow carefully all the words of this law." (Deuteronomy 31:10-12 NIV)

5) Witnesses. A list of those who can verify that the covenant has been carried out, or who will enforce it. Since a party to the covenant cannot also act as witness, God calls on the creation to fill the role. For example, "This day I call heaven and earth as witnesses against you…" (Deuteronomy 30:19 NIV)

6) Blessings and Curses. These are the benefits which the people will receive from keeping the covenant and the curses which will come on them if they don't (Leviticus 26, Deuteronomy 28).

There are two more important things to note about how the covenant was put into effect or sealed.

> 1) The blood of the covenant. "When Moses went and told the people all the LORD's words and laws, they responded with one voice, "Everything the LORD has said we will do." Moses then wrote down everything the LORD had said. He got up early the next morning and built an altar at the foot of the mountain and set up twelve stone pillars representing the twelve tribes of Israel. Then he sent young Israelite men, and they offered burnt offerings and sacrificed young bulls as fellowship offerings to the LORD. Moses took half of the blood and put it in bowls, and the other half he sprinkled on the altar. Then he took the Book of the Covenant and read it to the people. They responded, "We will do everything the LORD has said; we will obey." Moses then took the blood, sprinkled it on the people and said, "This is the blood of the covenant that the LORD has made with you in accordance with all these words."" (Exodus 24:3-8 NIV)

Once the people accepted the terms of the covenant, it was sealed or ratified with blood. Sprinkling blood on the alter indicated God's acceptance of the sacrifice. Sprinkling blood on the people cleansed them (purified them from sin) and marked them as belonging to God.

2) The covenant meal. Once the covenant was ratified, representatives of the people ate a meal in God's presence. "Moses and Aaron, Nadab and Abihu, and the seventy elders of Israel went up and saw the God of Israel. Under his feet was something like a pavement made of sapphire, clear as the sky itself. But God did not raise his hand against these leaders of the Israelites; they saw God, and they ate and drank." (Exodus 24:9-11 NIV) No doubt one of the purposes of a covenant meal was participation or fellowship between the parties to the covenant. (For example, see Genesis 31:53-54 and context.) The elders of Israel were fellowshipping with God.

V.   Parallels

The covenant which God made with the Israelites at Sinai was a forerunner of the much more significant covenant which God was going to offer mankind through Jesus Christ. The covenant made through Moses is called the Old Covenant, while the one made through Jesus is called the New Covenant. There are some remarkable parallels between the two.

1) It's God who makes the offer in both cases.

2) There were approximately 50 days between when the Israelites left Egypt and the Law was given at Mt. Sinai. There were 50 days between the Passover when Jesus was crucified and the New Covenant was proclaimed at Pentecost.

3) The Israelites had to demonstrate faith. They accepted God's offer before they knew the terms. We also have to believe and trust God in order to enter the New Covenant.

4) The Israelites needed a mediator. Jesus is the mediator of the New Covenant. "For there is one God and one mediator between God and men, the man Christ Jesus," (1 Timothy 2:5 NIV)

5) The Israelites had to wash their clothes – a symbol of renouncing sin. We also have to repent of sin before we can enter the New Covenant.

6) Both covenants required a sacrifice.

7) Just as the Israelites were sprinkled with the blood of the covenant, the blood of Christ must be applied to those entering the New Covenant. "The blood of goats and bulls and the ashes of a heifer sprinkled on those who are ceremonially unclean sanctify them so that they are outwardly clean. How much more, then, will the blood of Christ, who through the eternal Spirit offered himself unblemished to God, cleanse our consciences from acts that lead to death, so that we may serve the living God!" (Hebrews 9:13-14 NIV)

8) There is a covenant meal – the Lord's Supper or Communion. "Is not the cup of thanksgiving for which we give thanks a participation in the blood of Christ? And is not the bread that we break a participation in the body of Christ? Because there is one loaf, we, who are many, are one body, for we all partake of the one loaf." (1 Corinthians 10:16-17 NIV) "…The Lord Jesus, on the night he was betrayed, took bread, and when he had given thanks, he broke it and said, "This is my body, which is for you; do this in remembrance of me." In the same way, after supper he took the cup, saying, "This cup is the new covenant in my blood; do this, whenever you drink it, in remembrance of me."" (1 Corinthians 11:23-25 NIV)

9) Just as God viewed the Israelites as a kingdom of priests and a holy nation, those in the New Covenant are also a kingdom of priests and a holy nation (1 Peter 2:9-10). Just as the nation of Israel was intended to be a blessing to the rest of the world and was to show God's glory to them, those in the New Covenant are to declare God's praises.

What was the need for a New Covenant?

1) The people proved that they were unable to keep the Old Covenant. The Old Covenant was based on rules and regulations which no one aside from Christ was able to completely obey. In contrast, the New Covenant is based on a changed nature (Hebrews 8:7-13).

2) There was nothing in the Old Covenant which could take away sin. The sin sacrifices which were offered year after year, were really only sort of a promissory note. They deferred the reckoning another year. It is only in the New Covenant that the sacrifice of Christ pays the penalty of sin once for all (Hebrews 10:1-18).

૪૦૦૪

Highlights of the Law

Introduction: Every society needs a set of agreed-upon principles and rules in order to function. Whenever such rules do not exist, or people will not agree to live by them, chaos results. It doesn't matter whether the society in question is an individual home, a school, a business, a ship or an entire nation, if the principles and rules are not there and enforced, that society will soon self-destruct.

God offered to enter into a covenant relationship with the Israelite people. If they would enter this relationship, God promised that they would be a kingdom of priests and a holy nation (Exodus 19:5-6). That is, the Israelites would be chosen by God, above all other peoples and nations, in order to fulfill a special place and purpose in salvation history.

It's important to understand that the whole covenant relationship which God offered was based firmly on obedience. Notice the condition in Exodus 19:5, "Now if you obey me fully and keep my covenant, then…" (NIV).

Not only was obedience the condition of God's offer, the people fully understood that obedience was required. At least three times they declared, "…We will do everything the LORD has said…" (Exodus 19:8, 24:3, 7). By stating that they would obey, the people expressed agreement with the principles and rules that were going to govern the new community that God was going to bring into being through this covenant.

I.   The Lawgiver

Who is the person who determined what the principles and rules of the covenant between God and the Israelites would be?

> Though we often call it the 'Law of Moses,' in reality it was God who gave all the commandments. It was God who set the terms of the covenant. This is one of the things which makes the Law so different from the laws of other nations. In all cases, whether you talk about the laws of the Hittites, the Babylonians, the Egyptians or the law of Hammurabi, they

all were given by a king or some other human. But in the case of this covenant, the laws and statutes were given by God.

What are the implications of the Law being given by God rather than a human?

1) It is an expression of divine will. Since God does not change (Malachi 3:6), what this means is that the laws are absolute. There could be no negotiation. There could be questions about how to apply certain rules or regulations, but the rules, themselves, and the principles upon which they are based are absolute. Our culture has the idea that truth is relative. Truth depends on circumstances. What may be good for you is not necessarily what's good for me. In contrast to this way of thinking, the Law is universal and absolute.

2) Though the Law touches on many different areas of life, it is really something spiritual. It would be possible to keep every detail of the Law and still miss the whole point. It was this sort of legalism – which honored outward appearances but missed the true righteousness which God wanted which got Jesus so upset with the religious leaders of His day. "Woe to you, teachers of the law and Pharisees, you hypocrites! You give a tenth of your spices – mint, dill and cummin. But you have neglected the more important matters of the law – justice, mercy and faithfulness. You should have practiced the latter, without neglecting the former. You blind guides! You strain out a gnat but swallow a camel." (Matthew 23:23-24 NIV)

3) Because the Law was given by God and the purpose for it was to bind the people to Him in covenant relationship, the primary reason for keeping the Law should have been to please God. Yes, there were blessings promised for keeping it; yes, there were penalties for breaking the regulations, but the most important thing was the people's, and therefore the nation's, relationship with God. The Law was not intended as an end in itself, but the means to make it possible to be God's people.

II.   Ten Words (The 'Ten Commandments')

The Ten Commandments (literally the "Ten Words") are the heart of the Law. To a large extent, the rest of the regulations are an extension and expansion of the principles in the Ten Commandments. They are so important that God, Himself, wrote them out on stone and gave the stones to Moses (Exodus 24:12, 32:15-16). It was the Ten Commandments which were placed in the 'Ark of the Covenant' (Deuteronomy 10:5).

Though most of the Ten Commandments are expressed as a negative, "Do not" it is important to understand that the laws are really two-sided. In addition to refraining from doing a particular thing, the people were expected to do the opposite of what was prohibited. If all that was involved in keeping the Law was to not do, then all that would be needed to keep it would be to do nothing! That is not what God intended. For example, in order to really fulfill the commandment to not worship idols, it is necessary to give true worship – or, to express it another way, to worship God. As another example, the commandment to not give false testimony implies the obligation to give true testimony.

Why do you think most of the Ten Commandments are given in the form of "Do not"?

> Because it is easy to define what we should not do but there may be many different ways to fulfill the opposite good which is implied. For example, it is easy to define and understand what "Do not murder" means. But it is not so easy to define all the ways in which we can do the good which the commandment implies we ought to do. There are many different ways to bless or help someone.

Instead of looking at all ten of the commandments in detail, we're just going to mention some of the highlights.

> 1) Don't make idols. The key to this command is the idea of worship. God did not prohibit art, or even religious art. In fact, God instructed the people to weave a lot of images in the fabric walls of the tabernacle, which was the center of

worship for the nation. It's not art or images which God prohibited, but the worship of them.

It's easy to understand why it's not right to worship something in place of God, but why is it inappropriate to make an image or representation of God?

> The reason it is inappropriate to make a representation of God is that He is outside of, or beyond nature and time. Nature is a created thing. God is the Creator and is from eternity. He transcends nature. To make an image or representation of Him is to try to make Him part of nature. In effect, we try to lower Him and do not recognize Him as being above and beyond nature.

2) Don't take the Lord's name in vain. The NIV translation captures the idea when it says, "You shall not misuse the name of the Lord…" (Exodus 20:7)

How can we misuse God's name?

> Most people probably associate taking the Lord's name in vain, or misusing God's name with idle or casual swearing. This is certainly true, but there is a great deal more. We can understand this better when we stop and think about names. Names have meaning. They often express the nature or the character of the object or person which bears the name. Therefore, to misuse God's name is to associate one of His names with something which is contrary to His will or character. For example, God is good. When we do something evil in His name, we misuse His name.

Application: There is a very practical application of this principle for Christians. We bear Christ's name. Therefore we should live our lives as Christ would. We should think and act as He would. When we don't, we are misusing His name.

3) Don't commit adultery. Adultery always involves a sexual relationship with someone else's spouse or fiancée. In the Law, it always carried the death penalty. Other sexual sins sometimes had lesser penalties.

Why is adultery mentioned in the Ten Commandments and why was the penalty so drastic?

> Probably, the reason is that the whole idea of the Commandments was to establish a covenant relationship between God and the people. Adultery involves the violation of another covenant – the marriage covenant between a husband and wife. The marriage covenant pictures the relationship which people ought to have with God (For example, see Ephesians 5:22-33). Unfaithfulness to God is often referred to as spiritual adultery.

> Since a covenant is supposed to last until death, death is a fitting penalty for breaking it. The words "till death do us part" in a wedding ceremony are not meaningless. They bind the marriage partners to each other for their entire lives and imply that if the partners are not faithful to the marriage covenant then they are worthy of death. The words should not be spoken lightly.

Digression: Our culture encourages premarital and extramarital sex. In contrast to our culture, God intends for sexual conduct to take place exclusively within the marriage relationship. Within marriage, as God intends, sex is good, wholesome and holy. Outside of marriage, it is unholy and leads to all kinds of perversion. People should abstain before marriage in anticipation of entering into the marriage covenant. After marriage they should not break covenant by sexual activity outside the marriage.

Girls – one of the greatest gifts you can give to your husband is your virginity. Our culture tells you to use your body and sexuality to entice. But what you may not realize is that while men will use you, they do not respect or value those who flaunt themselves, dress immodestly or indulge in premarital sexual activity. One of the surest ways to lose the respect of someone worth marrying is to start sleeping around. If you don't want people to think of you and treat you as a slut, then don't behave like one. Do you want to be regarded as a sex object or as valuable and precious? Do you want to be cherished and respected? Then guard your bodies and do not involve yourself in any action with anyone that would lead to something which should take place only within marriage. You will never regret saving yourself for your husband. The world is filled with people who regret that they did not wait.

Guys – one of the greatest gifts you can give to your future wife is faithfulness. Be faithful to your marriage by remaining sexually pure before you enter into the marriage covenant. A woman needs security. It will give your wife a tremendous sense of security if she knows that you saved yourself for her. In contrast, if you are not faithful to the marriage beforehand, there will always be potential for a seed of doubt in your wife's mind whether you will be unfaithful after you are married.

God intended you to be leaders. It is you who generally take the lead in courtship. As such you have a huge responsibility toward the girls. To a large extent girls will, at least subconsciously, try to conform to your expectations. What values do you project? Do you value modesty and purity or do you encourage immodesty and lewd behavior? Do you treat girls as sex objects or do you treat them as princesses – children of the King of Kings? Do you guard their hearts and reputations or do you break their hearts and defile their reputations?

III.   Something Unique

Since the Law was given by God, and not by man, it is very, very different than the laws which governed the other nations. Here are some of the major differences:

> 1) The world says that religion and everyday life shouldn't mix. People put up a wall between what they call the secular and the sacred. The Law of Moses, in total contrast to other systems, makes no distinction between crime and sin. To

wrong someone is to sin against God also. This also introduces a different reason to keep the Law. The primary reason was not to avoid punishment, but to please God.

2) In contrast to other systems, the Law applied equally to everyone – regardless of social status or whether they were rich or poor. Other systems of law were put into place to guard the status of the nobles or the aristocracy. In contrast, the Law of Moses treated everyone the same – even aliens and foreigners who lived among the Israelites. For example, even slaves were guaranteed a day of rest like everyone else.

3) Punishment fit the crime.

> a) In other systems it was routine to punish family members along with the person who broke the law. The Law of Moses specifically forbade punishing anyone except the person who was guilty.

> **Question:** How can we reconcile this with God's words that He punishes the children for the sins of the fathers to the third or fourth generation (Exodus 20:5)?

>> First, consequences are not the same as holding someone guilty. For example, if a drunk comes home and beats his wife and children, they are not responsible for his behavior yet suffer the consequences of his behavior. In the same way, sin can affect three or four generations down-road. Secondly, thought patterns and attitudes get passed on to following generations. For example, there are many cases of families who live on welfare for generations. We often hear of the need to 'break the cycle' in regard to lifestyle and behavior patterns.

> b) Other systems of law had a built-in bias toward the rich through the use of monetary fines. The Law of

Moses is based on the principle of equivalence. Tooth for tooth, eye for eye, etc.

4) The Law of Moses always gives priority to people over property. Other systems place a higher value on property than on people.

5) Everyone had a duty to know the Law. It was to be read to the people every seven years. Fathers were to instruct their children in it. It was to be a daily topic of conversation. In other societies, ordinary people were forbidden to know or study the law. Knowledge of the law was restricted to the nobility or the priests.

IV.   Is the Law Still in Force?

In a sense, yes. God demands perfection. If someone were able to keep the Law perfectly, then God would accept him on the basis of a blameless life. But, aside from Jesus, no one has ever been able to keep the Law. So, what was intended to give life, actually became a cause of spiritual death. A better system, a New Covenant was needed.

Jesus fulfilled the Law (Matthew 5:17-18). Not, as some maintain, just the ceremonial parts of the Law, but all of it – including the Ten Commandments. True, Christians still live by some of the same principles as given in the Law of Moses but it is not because the Law is still in force, but because those principles have become part of the New Covenant.

Also, the New Covenant is on an entirely different basis than the Old. The Old Covenant was based on perfect obedience. It depended on human effort. The New Covenant is based on a changed nature. It does not depend on rules to modify behavior, but on a new nature which inherently wants to do what is right.

ଽଔଔ

Sacrifices and Festivals

Introduction: Along with the ethical teachings of the Law and the specific rules, there were rituals and holy days. It is the traditions and festivals which remind a group of their history and heritage. It is the traditions and festivals which embody the core values of the group.

I.   Sacrifices

Something which immediately stands out when reading the Law is the incredible number of sacrifices which were required. Thousands upon thousands of animals were slaughtered each year in the rituals. One common theme in all of the animal sacrifices is atonement. The animal was a substitute for the life of the individual who offered it. A person's sin and guilt was symbolically transferred to the animal before its life was offered to God. The principle of life for life was graphically illustrated by sprinkling or applying some of the blood on the altar, or pouring it out at the base of the altar. Hebrews 9:22 explains it this way: "…the law requires that nearly everything be cleansed with blood, and without the shedding of blood there is no forgiveness." (NIV)

1)   Burnt Offering (Leviticus 1:1-17, 6:8-13)

The entire body of the animal was burnt in this offering. It symbolized the complete dedication or offering of oneself to God. There was also the idea of substitution. The person making the offering would place his hand on the animal's head before it was killed. God would then accept the animal in atonement for the person who offered it. In addition to the burnt offerings made by individuals, they were made for the entire nation every morning and evening.

2)   Grain Offering (Leviticus 2:1-16, 6:14-23)

A portion of the grain offerings were burnt on the altar. The remainder was given to the priests. Since the priests did not have any farm land of their own, the grain offerings were one way in which they got their food.

3)   Fellowship or Peace Offering (Leviticus 3:1-17, 7:11-38)

As the name implies, the main idea behind the fellowship or peace offerings was to express and deepen relationships. There are two aspects to fellowship: the horizontal relationship with family members and friends or other members of the community, and the vertical relationship with God. In this offering, only the fat and certain internal organs were burned. A portion of the meat was given to the priests. The rest of the animal was eaten by the worshipers. It was sort of a sacred barbecue – a time for families to draw closer to one another as well as to God; a time of communion.

4)   Sin Offering (Leviticus 4:1-5:13, 6:24-30)

The sin offering was intended to cover general sin. That is, sin which was not a conscious and deliberate rebellion against God. These were sins of oversight, carelessness and ignorance. Sin offerings could be made by individuals. At certain times sin offerings were made for the entire nation.

5)   Guilt Offering (Leviticus 5:14-6:7, 7:1-10)

The guilt offering is similar to the sin offering except it was for those sins which required restitution. In other words, it was for those sins which involved the misuse of someone else's property or goods. Along with the offering, a fine was paid.

Even though God required all these sacrifices, they were inadequate to really take away sin. The basic problem is that no animal has the same value as a human being. Something better was needed. This is why Jesus' sacrifice of Himself for us is so important. Hebrews 10 explains.

[read Hebrews 10:1-12]

II.   Holy Days

The 7ᵗʰ day of every week (Saturday) was to be a Sabbath, that is a day of rest. It is a reminder of God resting after the six days of creation. On the first day of every month, that is every new moon (the Israelites followed a lunar calendar), there were special sacrifices. In addition to these weekly and monthly celebrations, there were several major holy days or festivals throughout the year.

1)   Passover (Feast of Unleavened Bread) and Firstfruits
      (Leviticus 23:4-14)

Passover is the 1st of 3 pilgrimage festivals when the men were supposed to travel to where the tabernacle/temple was. It was celebrated on the 14th day of the first month of the religious calendar. (Sometime during our April or May.) It was a remembrance and celebration of delivery from bondage in Egypt. This festival is called Passover because the angel of death 'passed over' the Israelite houses which had the blood of the Passover lamb applied to the posts and lintels of the door. Closely associated with Passover is the idea of redemption. Since the first-born of the Egyptians died during the night of the first Passover, the Israelites were commanded to redeem their first-born by substituting a lamb.

Since the Passover celebration took place at the beginning of the harvest season, the firstfruits, or the first sheaves of grain were offered to the Lord two days after Passover. (That is on the 16th of the month.)

2)   Feast of Weeks (Pentecost) (Leviticus 23:15-22)

50 days after Passover, they celebrated the end of the harvest. The Feast of Weeks is the 2nd of the 3 pilgrimage festivals. Not only was the harvest celebrated, but part of it was set aside for the poor. It is interesting to note that since the destruction of the Temple in 70 AD, Pentecost has also become a memorial of the giving of the Law at Sinai.

3)   Feast of Trumpets (Rosh Hashanah) (Leviticus 23:23-
      25)

This marked the first day of the civil calendar (New Year's Day). It was the first day of the seventh month of the religious calendar and corresponds to our September or October. It was a day of rest.

4)   Day of Atonement (Yom Kippur) (Leviticus 16:1-34, 23:26-32)

The 10th day of the seventh month was the most solemn day of the entire year. Everyone was to fast, abstain from all work and repent of wrongdoing. Anyone who refused to fast was supposed to be cut off from his people. To express it another way, a person was excluded from citizenship in the nation. On this day the High Priest would offer a sin offering on behalf of the nation. They would also symbolically transfer the sins of the people to a goat which would then be released into the wilderness. This goat is called the "scapegoat."

5)   Feast of Tabernacles (Booths) (Leviticus 23:33-44)

The day of solemn repentance on the 10th of the seventh month was followed by a week of rejoicing which began on the 15th day of the month. This was the 3rd of the 3 annual pilgrimage feasts in the Jewish year. People were supposed to travel from their homes to wherever the tabernacle/temple was. The first and eighth days of this festival were days of rest. For the entire week, the people were supposed to live in shelters constructed for the occasion. This was a national camp-out. It commemorated the wanderings in the wilderness after God rescued the nation from slavery in Egypt. It was a Thanksgiving festival. The Puritans probably had this festival in mind when they instituted what became the American Thanksgiving holiday.

Application: Just as the sacrifices pointed forward to the perfect sacrifice of Christ, the festivals also pointed forward to the blessings we celebrate in Christ.

1) We look forward to a Sabbath rest in heaven (Hebrews 4:1-11).

2) Jesus is called our Passover lamb (1 Corinthians 5:7-8, 1 Peter 1:14-19). He was crucified at the time of Passover. Just as the blood of the Passover lamb protected the Israelites, Christ's blood protects us from the destroyer. Just as the Passover is a reminder of deliverance from slavery in Egypt, we are reminded each week of our deliverance from the bondage of sin when we participate in the Lord's Supper. Just as the lamb had to be without defect, we also are to be holy.

3) Jesus is called the firstfruits. This is a reference to His resurrection from the dead. His victory over death gives us hope and assurance that some day we also will be resurrected (1 Corinthians 15:19-23).

4) Just as the Feast of Weeks took place fifty days after the Passover and is a reminder that the Law was given approximately 50 days after leaving Egypt, the church came into existence 50 days after Christ's death (Acts 2:1-41).

5) Both repentance and thanksgiving are part of becoming and remaining a Christian.

III.   National Festivals

In addition to the holy days and festivals which are listed in the Law, there are two festivals which were added later in celebration of special events in Israel's history.

1)   Purim

Purim commemorates the deliverance of the Jews from annihilation in the time of Queen Esther. (See Esther 9:20-32.)

2)   Feast of Dedication (Hanukkah)

This feast commemorates the re-dedication of the Temple after it had been defiled by the Syrians during the period between the Old and New Testaments. It is mentioned in John 10:22.

IV.   Special Years

1)   Sabbatical Year (Leviticus 25:1-7)

The people were to rest every 7 days. But there was another type of rest as well. Every 7th year, the people were to give the land rest. They were to let their fields go fallow. God promised that if they would do this, He would provide enough during the 6th year to see them through till the harvest of the 8th year. Not only was the land to be given rest, all debts were to be forgiven and all slaves set free.

2)   Jubilee (Leviticus 25:8-34)

The 50th year was a special year. Not only was it a Sabbatical year in which debts were canceled and slaves set free, all farm and pasture land was to be returned to the original owner or his heirs. In this way, ancestral homesteads stayed in the family. No matter how badly someone had fouled up, he got a chance to start over.

Application: The Sabbatical year and the Year of Jubilee emphasize the concepts of rest, forgiveness, freedom and redemption. All of these find their fulfillment in Christ.

ഇൻ൫

The Tabernacle
(Exodus 25:1-31:11, 35:4-40:33)

Introduction: Not only did the Law of Moses contain rules for living as well as instructions for various sacrifices and festivals, it also contained detailed plans for building a movable tent for a place of worship. We call this tent, and its surrounding courtyard, the Tabernacle.

However, the Tabernacle is far more than a place of worship. It has a far deeper meaning. It is also a visible metaphor of how to worship. It is a graphic illustration of the process and means by which sinful people may approach a holy God.

In addition to being a place of worship and an illustration of how we can approach God, the Tabernacle also looked far to the future. It was a symbol of a greater reality. It pointed to the church and also to heaven itself. Because of this, it has great meaning for us today.

I.   Arrangement Of The Tabernacle

The Courtyard of the Tabernacle was a rectangle about 150 feet long by 75 feet wide. Another way to envision it is two 75 foot squares put together. The long side of the Tabernacle ran east and west with the entrance on the east side.

In the middle of the first square of the Courtyard stood the Altar of Burnt Offering. Between this altar and the second square was a large water basin called the Laver. This is where the priests washed before presenting offerings on the altar and before entering the Tabernacle proper.

In the second square of the Courtyard was a tent approximately 45 feet long, 15 feet wide and 15 feet high. It was divided into two sections. The first section was 30 feet long. It was called the Holy Place. On the right as you went in, that is along the north wall, was a table called the Table of Shewbread. On it the 'Bread of the Presence' was placed every week.

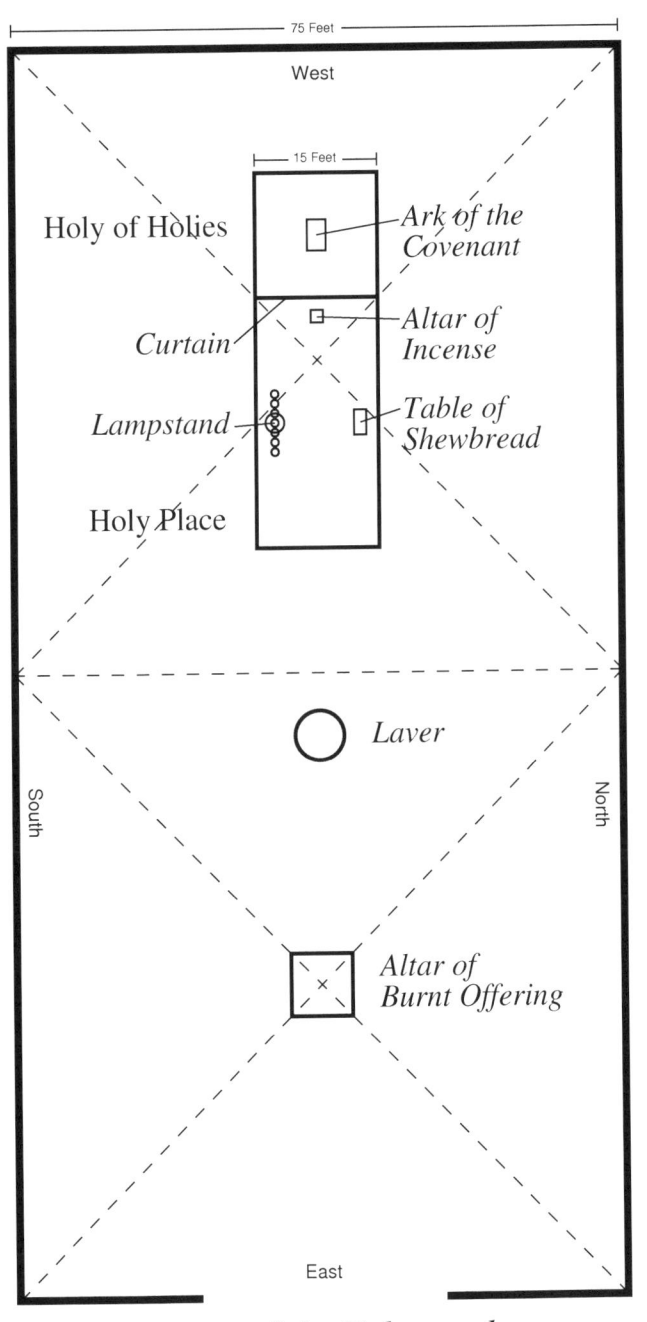

Layout of the Tabernacle

Opposite the table, along the south wall, was a golden Lampstand. In front of the Curtain which divided the Holy Place from the last section of the Tabernacle was the Altar of Incense.

A curtain (also called the 'Veil') separated the Holy Place from the last section of the Tabernacle. This latter was a cube-shaped room which was 15 feet in all directions. In it was the Ark of the Covenant. This was the box or chest in which the stone tablets were kept on which God had inscribed the Ten Commandments. The lid of the ark was made of gold. This lid was called the Mercy Seat. On it were two cherubim fashioned out of hammered gold. They faced toward each other while looking down at the Mercy Seat. Their wings were outstretched. God placed His Presence between these two cherubim. The Bible pictures God as 'enthroned on the cherubim' (1 Samuel 4:4, 2 Kings 19:15, Psalm 80:11, etc.).

II.   Progression Of Holiness

Any Israelite could enter the Courtyard. But only priests could enter the Holy Place. In other words, only those who had been specially consecrated or set apart to serve God at the Tabernacle could go into the Holy Place. Even the priests had to wash at the Laver before they could enter.

Only the High Priest was allowed to enter the Holy of Holies where God's Presence was. He was permitted to enter once a year, on the Day of Atonement, with the blood from the sin offering. He would sprinkle the blood on the Mercy Seat and God would accept the blood in atonement for the sins of the people for one more year.

The arrangement of the Tabernacle, with its progression from the common to the consecrated to the infinite holiness of God, parallels the situation at Mt. Sinai during the giving of the Law. There the people were gathered in front of the mountain. The Elders of the people were allowed to come to the foot or base of the mountain while only Moses was allowed to climb the mountain where God's Presence was.

III.   Picture Of What Was To Come

The Old Covenant was centered on the Tabernacle (and later, the Temple) where the record of the Law was kept, and where the sacrifices specified in the Law were made. But the Tabernacle also prefigured the New Covenant. There is deep symbolism in each part of it. All of it points to Christ and His redeeming work.

What does it all mean?

1) The Courtyard represents the world.

2) The Holy Place represents the church. "…you are no longer foreigners and aliens, but fellow citizens with God's people and members of God's household, built on the foundation of the apostles and prophets, with Christ Jesus himself as the chief cornerstone. In him the whole building is joined together and rises to become a holy temple in the Lord. And in him you too are being built together to become a dwelling in which God lives by his Spirit." (Ephesians 2:19-22 NIV)

3) The Holy of Holies represents heaven. "For Christ did not enter a man-made sanctuary that was only a copy of the true one; he entered heaven itself, now to appear for us in God's presence. Nor did he enter heaven to offer himself again and again, the way the high priest enters the Most Holy Place every year with blood that is not his own. Then Christ would have had to suffer many times since the creation of the world. But now he has appeared once for all at the end of the ages to do away with sin by the sacrifice of himself." (Hebrews 9:24-26 NIV)

Just as the Tabernacle structure pointed to something much more significant, so too do the furnishings. Beginning at the entrance of the Tabernacle and moving forward:

1) The Altar of Burnt Offering points to the sacrifice of Christ. "He is the atoning sacrifice for our sins, and not only for ours but also for the sins of the whole world." (1 John 2:2 NIV)

2) The Laver points to baptism. Just as the priests purified themselves before entering the Holy Place by washing the dirt from their feet and hands, we are purified through baptism so we can enter the church. In a different context Peter writes, "and this water symbolizes baptism that now saves you also – not the removal of dirt from the body but the pledge of a good conscience toward God. It saves you by the resurrection of Jesus Christ," (1 Peter 3:21 NIV)

3) The Lampstand represents God's Word. "Your word is a lamp to my feet and a light for my path." (Psalm 119:105 NIV) Because the Word gives light, those who live it and proclaim it illuminate the world. Jesus told His disciples, "You are the light of the world..." (Matthew 5:14 NIV) And Paul writes, "Do everything without complaining or arguing, so that you may become blameless and pure, children of God without fault in a crooked and depraved generation, in which you shine like stars in the universe as you hold out the word of life..." (Philippians 2:14-16 NIV) Churches are also called lampstands in Revelation 1:20.

4) The Altar of Incense represents the prayers of Christians. Compare the following verses: "...the four living creatures and the twenty-four elders fell down before the Lamb. Each one had a harp and they were holding golden bowls full of incense, which are the prayers of the saints." (Revelation 5:8 NIV) "Another angel, who had a golden censer, came and stood at the altar. He was given much incense to offer, with the prayers of all the saints, on the golden altar before the throne. The smoke of the incense, together with the prayers of the saints, went up before God from the angel's hand." (Revelation 8:3-4 NIV)

5) The Table of Shewbread points to Jesus who is the bread of life. Jesus said, "I am the living bread that came down from heaven. If anyone eats of this bread, he will live forever. This bread is my flesh, which I will give for the life of the world." (John 6:51 NIV) In the Tabernacle the bread was eaten once a week. It is quite likely that the first

Christians used this as their example when they celebrated the Lord's Supper or Communion, once a week on the Lord's Day.

The unleavened bread is also a metaphor for the kind of life Christians are supposed to live. The bread represents Christians either individually or as a group, while leaven or yeast represents sin. "Your boasting is not good. Don't you know that a little yeast works through the whole batch of dough? Get rid of the old yeast that you may be a new batch without yeast – as you really are. For Christ, our Passover lamb, has been sacrificed. Therefore let us keep the Festival, not with the old yeast, the yeast of malice and wickedness, but with bread without yeast, the bread of sincerity and truth." (1 Corinthians 5:6-8 NIV)

6) The Veil is a representation of the separation there is between God and man. Matthew 27:51, Mark 15:38 and Luke 23:45 record that when Jesus died the veil or curtain of the Temple, which was a permanent replacement for the Tabernacle, was torn in two. This pointed to the fact that through Jesus, we now have access to God. "...we have confidence to enter the Most Holy Place by the blood of Jesus, by a new and living way opened for us through the curtain, that is, his body," (Hebrews 10:19-20 NIV) "... through him we both have access to the Father by one Spirit." (Ephesians 2:18 NIV)

7) The Mercy Seat is where God's righteousness and love came into contact. God's Law which condemned sinners, and God's Love which wanted to save them were both satisfied by the blood of the sin offering which was sprinkled on the Mercy Seat. The animal sacrifices which were offered under the Old Covenant were really just promissory notes pointing to the perfect sacrifice which would meet our need. Jesus made that perfect sacrifice. "He did not enter by means of the blood of goats and calves; but he entered the Most Holy Place once for all by his own blood, having obtained eternal redemption. The blood of goats and bulls and the ashes of a

heifer sprinkled on those who are ceremonially unclean sanctify them so that they are outwardly clean. How much more, then, will the blood of Christ, who through the eternal Spirit offered himself unblemished to God, cleanse our consciences from acts that lead to death, so that we may serve the living God!" (Hebrews 9:12-14 NIV) "for all have sinned and fall short of the glory of God, and are justified freely by his grace through the redemption that came by Christ Jesus. God presented him as a sacrifice of atonement, through faith in his blood. He did this to demonstrate his justice, because in his forbearance he had left the sins committed beforehand unpunished – he did it to demonstrate his justice at the present time, so as to be just and the one who justifies those who have faith in Jesus." (Romans 3:23-26 NIV)

Though we should be careful not to read too much into the the arrangement of the Tabernacle and its furnishings, it is interesting to note that if you draw lines between the furnishings, they form the shape of a cross. In any case, the only way we can approach God is by means of Christ's sacrifice. We must be baptized in order to enter the Holy Place, that is the church. Once we enter, the Word gives us light, we commune with Christ by eating the bread of life and we offer prayers to God. Because of Christ's blood we now have access to the Most Holy Place, that is heaven, where God sits on His throne.

IV.   Make All Things According To The Pattern

Something that we need to keep in mind is that it is God who set the terms of the Old Covenant. Moses was not free to make the Tabernacle any way he wanted. God gave specific instructions for the Tabernacle and its furnishings. "See that you make them according to the pattern shown you on the mountain." (Exodus 25:40 NIV)

Application: In the same way, it is God who set the terms of New Covenant. There are many who try to tamper with the conditions. There are many who try to change the terms to suit their own whims. But just as Moses was not free to tamper with the design of the

Tabernacle, we are not free to tamper with the terms of salvation or the design of the church. We, too, must follow the pattern which God has shown us in the New Testament.

かく

Covenant Broken and Renewed
(Exodus 32:1-35, Leviticus 10:1-20)

Introduction: The Israelites had entered into a covenant relationship with God. A covenant not only contains promises, it has terms. The covenant must be kept in order for the blessings to come about. The people had committed themselves to do everything that God required of them. But things don't always go according to our expectations. Sometimes it takes longer than we would like before we reap the benefits we expected. The Israelites got tired of waiting.

I.   This Fellow Moses (Exodus 32:1)

What were the causes of the Israelites' frustration?

> 1) Moses was a long time coming down from the mountain. A lapse in leadership causes uncertainty. In Moses' absence, Aaron should have taken charge and given the people reassurance. Apparently he did not and the people were confused about who would lead them in further travels.

> 2) They had a basic contempt for Moses and his leadership. This is evident from their calling him "this fellow." They apparently cared more for the things Moses could do for them than they did for him as a person and the role which God had given him.

Lesson: God wants us to have a genuine respect for our spiritual leaders. "Now we ask you, brothers, to respect those who work hard among you, who are over you in the Lord and who admonish you. Hold them in the highest regard in love because of their work..." (1 Thessalonians 5:12-13 NIV) Whenever we develop the attitude of "What's in it for me?" we are setting ourselves up to fall.

II.   These Are Your Gods (Exodus 32:2-6)

In what way did the people's demand violate the covenant with God?

The very first of the Ten Commandments was, "You shall have no other gods before me." (Exodus 20:3 NIV) The second was, "You shall not make for yourself an idol…" (Exodus 20:4 NIV) By telling Aaron to make gods for them, they were breaking the most fundamental commands. It was these commands upon which the entire covenant was premised.

What was Aaron's response to the people's demand?

1) He temporized. Instead of taking a moral stand and calling the people back to obedience to the covenant, he tried to get off the hook by putting a high price tag on what they wanted. He told the people to provide the gold for the idol.

2) He tried to compromise. When the people called his bluff by giving him their gold earrings, Aaron made the idol, but he also built an altar and said that they were going to hold a festival to the Lord.

Application: There are still lots of people who try to do the same thing. They think that acknowledging God in some fashion gives them a license to live their lives any way they want. Go to church on Sunday and do what you want the rest of the week.

Lesson: Moral compromise never works. God is a jealous God in the sense that He does not tolerate any competition. He wants all or nothing. He will not share our hearts with anything else. Time after time in Scripture people are called upon to make a choice. Will they serve God, or will they not? "Now fear the LORD and serve him with all faithfulness. Throw away the gods your forefathers worshiped beyond the River and in Egypt, and serve the LORD. But if serving the LORD seems undesirable to you, then choose for yourselves this day whom you will serve, whether the gods your forefathers served beyond the River, or the gods of the Amorites, in whose land you are living. But as for me and my household, we will serve the LORD." (Joshua 24:14-15 NIV)

"Elijah went before the people and said, "How long will you waver between two opinions? If the LORD is God, follow him; but if Baal is God, follow him." But the people said nothing." (1 Kings 18:21 NIV)

Note: The idol Aaron made was in the shape of a calf. He probably modeled it after the Egyptian cow goddess, Hathor.

III.   Remember Your Servants (Exodus 32:7-14)

What was God's reaction to what the people did?

> 1) He disowned them. In verse 7 He refers to them as Moses' people instead of His own. One consequence of breaking covenant is that it severs the relationship between the parties who were in the covenant bond.

> 2) He wanted to destroy them. In place of the Israelites He offered to make a great nation from Moses' descendants.

On what basis did Moses ask God to relent?

> 1) To destroy the people would reflect badly on God's reputation. Other nations would say that God had evil or ulterior motives for taking the Israelites out of Egypt.

> 2) He asked God to remember the promises He had made to the patriarchs. Even if God did make a great nation out of Moses' descendants (Moses was an Israelite, too), on the surface it would not look like God had kept His promises to Abraham, Isaac and Jacob.

IV.   Running Wild (Exodus 32:15-29)

What were the people doing when Moses came down from the mountain?

> They were running wild (Exodus 32:25). Included in this was indulging in revelry (Exodus 32:6). Though it doesn't really come out in English translation, what this means is that there was an orgy going on, complete with sexual promiscuity and perversion.

Lesson: Whenever people turn their backs on God's covenant, it almost always leads to sexual promiscuity.

What was Moses' reaction when he witnessed what was going on?

> 1) He broke the stone tablets on which God had engraved the Ten Commandments.
>
> 2) He destroyed the idol, ground it to powder, mixed the powder into the water supply and forced the Israelites to drink the water.
>
> 3) He separated out those who were still loyal to God and had them kill the worst offenders.

What excuse did Aaron give for what he had done?

> 1) He tried to pass the buck by blaming the people.
>
> 2) He tried to minimize his own role by claiming that the idol had somehow just come into being by itself.

Lesson: When we do what is wrong, we need to learn to take responsibility for what we've done. Instead of making excuses, we need to repent.

V.   Whoever Has Sinned (Exodus 32:30-35)

How did Moses appeal to God for forgiveness for the people?

> He asked God to remove his own name from the book of life if God would not forgive. This is very similar to what Paul writes concerning the Jewish people of his day. "I have great sorrow and unceasing anguish in my heart. For I could wish that I myself were cursed and cut off from Christ for the sake of my brothers, those of my own race, the people of Israel..." (Romans 9:2-4 NIV)

What was God's response to Moses' plea?

> God responded that only the guilty would be removed from the book of life. This is a practical application of a principle that God had already stated in the Law. No one should be punished for a crime he has not committed.

VI.   Strange Fire (Leviticus 10:1-20)

At Mt. Sinai the people sinned by breaking the terms of the covenant. But there is another way to break covenant – by trying to change the terms.

What did Nadab and Abihu do?

> They lit their censors, and apparently the altar of incense, with unauthorized fire. The Law was very specific that the incense was to be lit from fire taken from the altar of burnt offering. (See Leviticus 16:12.)

What happened as a result?

> God killed them.

Lesson: God doesn't appreciate it when we make changes in the way He's told us to do things.

ഓൻൽ

Burdens of Leadership
(Numbers 11:1 – 12:16)

Introduction: The nation of Israel stayed at Mt. Sinai for about a year. During that time, they entered into covenant relationship with God, they bound themselves to obey the Law which God revealed through Moses, and they built the Tabernacle which was the focus of their national worship. The time at Mt. Sinai reconfirmed the Israelites as God's chosen people and transformed them into a nation.

Now it was time to move on. The emphasis shifts from organization to fulfilling the promise which God had given to bring them into the land of Canaan (Palestine). The immediate goal after leaving Egypt had been to arrive at Sinai. Now, the goal was to reach their permanent home in the Promised Land.

Though it is a relatively short distance from Sinai to the Land of Canaan, the journey was to prove a severe test of leadership. By studying what happened, we can learn some principles of leadership which are still valid today in the church.

I.   Ministry Of Intercession (Numbers 11:1-3)

The people had only traveled for three days (see Numbers 10:33) when the complaints started.

What was the reason for the complaints? (Numbers 11:1)

> The people complained about the hardships they were experiencing.

Lesson: Whenever we start concentrating on the journey and the hardships involved, rather than the goal and the blessings which God has promised, our situation will appear to be far worse than it actually is. We will begin to doubt the goodness of God and forget all the blessings He has already provided.

What did the people do when they began to reap the consequences of their grumbling? (Numbers 11:2)

They appealed to Moses, who then prayed to the Lord on their behalf. One of the characteristics of a true leader is that he has a genuine concern for the people under his care. He serves them. He looks out for their interests. Jesus said, "… You know that the rulers of the Gentiles lord it over them, and their high officials exercise authority over them. Not so with you. Instead, whoever wants to become great among you must be your servant, and whoever wants to be first must be your slave – just as the Son of Man did not come to be served, but to serve, and to give his life as a ransom for many." (Matthew 20:25-28 NIV)

Application: Moses could have told the people that they were getting what they deserved. But he didn't do that. Instead, he prayed for them. In the same way, prayer is one of the responsibilities of leaders in the church. For example, the Apostles delegated benevolence to others so that they could spend time in prayer (Acts 6:1-6). Intercessory prayer is also one of the responsibilities of Elders (James 5:13-20).

II.   You Can't Do It Alone (Numbers 11:4-35)

The grumbling in Numbers 11:1 was not specific. It was about the hardships in general. But now Moses was faced with something much more serious. Not only was there a specific complaint, it soon spread to the whole camp.

Who were the people who started the complaint? (Numbers 11:4)

It was the rabble, or mixed crowd, who had come with the Israelites when they left Egypt (see Exodus 12:38). These people apparently were not descendants of Abraham and, presumably, did not enter into the covenant with God at Mt. Sinai.

Lesson: We need to be careful who we associate with. God's people are to be separate from the surrounding culture. If we take up with ungodly people, or allow them to take up with us, there is a danger that we will adopt their values (see 1 Corinthians 15:33). In this case, the complaint started with the alien rabble but soon spread to every family among the Israelites (Numbers 11:10).

What was the basis of the complaint?

> It was that the food God had provided wasn't good enough. They wanted meat. They missed the fish, vegetables and melons they had eaten in Egypt. Notice how they romanticized their life in Egypt: We ate this stuff for free! (Numbers 11:5) In reality the life that these people had back in Egypt was not nearly as wonderful as they made it out to be. If life was so good, why had they left? They must have been looking for something better than what they had in Egypt.

Lesson: When we compare the "good old days" to the present what we are really doing is idealizing the past or, comparing the best of the past to the worst of the present.

> 1) It's okay to ask questions.

It's obvious that Moses was deeply discouraged and depressed by this situation. He vented his frustration in a series of questions. Notice that God did not become angry with Moses for voicing his discouragement and frustration. But it's extremely important to notice to whom Moses took his frustrations. Moses brought his frustrations to the Lord (Numbers 11:11). We see the same kind of thing in many of the Psalms. Where we get into trouble is when we vent to people rather than taking our troubles to God.

2) The burden is too heavy for one person.

Moses felt that the problem was far too big for him to handle (Numbers 11:14). The task of leadership is not easy. Part of leadership is administrative decision making. This in itself can be a huge responsibility. Then there is arbitration and problem solving. Remember that people brought their cases to Moses for him to decide. But more than anything, if you care about the people for whom you are responsible, leadership exacts a huge emotional and spiritual toll. If you don't have some way to refresh or restore your own spiritual reservoirs, the burden can break you. Burnout in ministry is a real possibility. You get so involved in tending to the needs of others and finding solutions to problems that there is no time or opportunity to tend to your own needs. Moses had reached the end of his spiritual and emotional tether. He asked God to either fix the situation or to kill him. For things to remain as they were was unbearable.

3) The principle of multiple leaders (Numbers 11:16-17).

Back in Exodus, chapter 18, at Jethro's suggestion, God had provided Moses with help with the administrative and judicial aspects of his task. At Sinai, many of the religious duties were delegated to the Levites in their capacity as priests. Now God provides Moses help with the spiritual and emotional part of the job. God gave the Spirit to seventy of Israel's elders.

Lesson: God does not intend for one person to bear the burdens of leadership alone. This principle is carried into the New Testament as well. Paul appointed, or made provisions for the appointment of Elders (plural) in each church. (For example, see Acts 14:23 and Titus 1:5.) These Elders were not a board of business managers, as is so often the case today. Instead they actively taught the people. They were the spiritual shepherds and overseers of the congregations. The New Testament knows nothing of the one-man 'Pastor' system which is so prevalent today. Instead, each congregation had multiple Pastors in their Elders. Perhaps there would be less leadership burnout if we went back to the the early church practice of sharing the task among several people.

4) Recognize the gifts of others (Numbers 11:26-30).

One obstacle to implementing multiple leadership is that leaders are reluctant to recognize the gifts and talents of others. They tend to think that no one can do as good a job as themselves. Or, they may be reluctant to share leadership roles with others because of insecurity – they are afraid that others will prove more talented than themselves and make them look bad. Moses had no such thoughts. He was thrilled that God had granted the gift of prophecy to others. Would that all leaders had the attitude of John the Baptist, "He must become greater; I must become less." (John 3:30 NIV)

Tangent: What is a prophet? The popular definition of prophecy is foretelling the future. While prophecy may involve foretelling, a more accurate concept is forth-telling, or proclaiming what God has said. A prophet is someone who speaks on behalf of God.

One reason for having multiple leaders is that no one has all the gifts and talents the church needs. God has gifted each one of us differently (Romans 12:3-8, 1 Corinthians 12:1-30). When people with different gifts work together in leadership, their strengths complement each other, and they can help compensate for each other's weaknesses.

5) Consequences of rejecting what God has provided (Numbers 11:31-34).

One of the burdens of leadership is watching people reap the consequences of their choice to turn away from what is right and/or insisting on having their own way. The people had complained about the manna God gave them for food. They demanded meat. Not only did their complaining discourage Moses, it had an unexpected consequence: God gave them meat, but He also sent a plague with it.

In referring to this incident Psalm 106 says, "In the desert they gave in to their craving; in the wasteland they put God to the test. So he gave them what they asked for, but sent a wasting disease upon them." (Psalm 106:14-15 NIV)

Lesson: If we complain, and pester God to do something long enough, He may eventually grant our request, but we won't like it when He does. There are always unexpected consequences when we go against God's will.

III.   Jealousy (Numbers 12:1-15)

Becoming a leader automatically makes you a target. Nails that stick up will get hammered! Not only will people dump their problems on you, you also become fair game for criticism. People will not like some of the decisions you make. They will press you to take actions that you think are unwise. When you do act, they will think that you should have done things differently.

But perhaps one of the biggest trials is people who are jealous of you and the ministry God has given you. It especially hurts when these people are among those who are closest to you. In this case, the ones who started to criticize Moses were from his own family. Since Miriam is listed first, it seems like she is the one who initiated the criticism and got Aaron to go along with it and back her up.

1) There will always be people who resent your role.

God selects people to do certain tasks. He gives particular spiritual gifts to one person and not another. The problem comes when we start to compare ourselves with others. This can take two forms:

a) How come he gets to do that (or how come he has that gift) and I don't?

b) I'm just as talented as he is. I'm involved in the same kind of ministry as he is. Why should he be the leader and not me?

It was the second of these comparisons that Aaron and Miriam made. "Has the LORD spoken only through Moses? … Hasn't he also spoken through us?…" (Numbers 12:2 NIV)

Lesson: The only way to be content is to realize that God has a place and a purpose for each one of us and He has gifted us all accordingly. We need to fulfill our task, not someone else's. If we force ourselves into a role God intends for someone else, it won't be a good fit and we won't be happy.

2) If they can't criticize your work, they will criticize you and your character.

On what did Miriam and Aaron base their criticism of Moses?

> Miriam and Aaron obviously knew that God had chosen Moses. They knew that he was acting in the capacity that God had assigned him. Since they couldn't criticize Moses for not doing the work God gave him, they went after his character. They complained that he wasn't fit to lead because of his home life.

> God did not agree with their assessment and struck Miriam with leprosy for her attitude and presumption.

Lesson: People will look for ways to criticize and discredit. We should make sure that we don't give them unnecessary opportunities to do so, particularly in the areas of morality and lifestyle. For example, one of the qualifications of an Elder in the church is that he must be 'above reproach' or 'blameless' in regard to his family and sexuality (see 1 Timothy 3:2, Titus 1:6).

෪෬

Too Much Of A Good Thing?
(Numbers 13:1-14:45, Deuteronomy 1:19-46)

Introduction: After all their trials, triumphs, complaints, rebellion and restoration, the Israelites finally came to the border of the land God had promised them. Quite naturally, they were curious about this land. What sort of place were they going to? What could they expect? What sort of people lived there? In order to find out, Moses chose 12 men, one from each of the tribes except Levi, and sent them into Canaan in order to get the answers. Their report, and the recommendation they made were to have a major impact on the history of Israel.

I.   A Survey Party (Numbers 13:1-20, Deuteronomy 1:19-23)

Whose idea was it to send in a survey team to scout out the land?

Numbers 13:1 says that God told Moses to select some men to explore the land. In Deuteronomy 1:22, however, we learn that the people urged Moses to send out spies. Putting the two accounts together, it seems that the people were the ones who made the request, and God graciously agreed to it.

What instructions did the scouts receive? (Numbers 13:18-20)

There were two major thrusts to the survey.

1) The scouts were to find out about the people. Were the people numerous, or was the land sparsely settled? Were they strong or weak? Were the towns fortified or not?

2) What kind of land was it? Was it fertile? Was it forested?

While a good case could be made for scouting out the land from the standpoint of determining routes, campsites and all the other details which are important in moving a large number of people into unfamiliar territory, the instructions to find out about the people and whether the land was good or bad seems odd. Hadn't God already told the Israelites about the peoples who lived there and that He would drive the inhabitants out before them? Hadn't God already told the

Israelites that it was good land? When God first commissioned Moses to rescue the people from Egyptian slavery this is what He said, "So I have come down to rescue them from the hand of the Egyptians and to bring them up out of that land into a good and spacious land, a land flowing with milk and honey–the home of the Canaanites, Hittites, Amorites, Perizzites, Hivites and Jebusites." (Exodus 3:8 NIV)

Application: Do we question what God tells us? Do we have to see before we will believe? Remember what Jesus said to Thomas after Thomas had said he would not believe the resurrection until he had put his fingers into Christ's wounds. "Then Jesus told him, "Because you have seen me, you have believed; blessed are those who have not seen and yet have believed."" (John 20:29 NIV)

II.   Explorers' Report (Numbers 13:21-14:4, Deuteronomy 1:24-28)

The whole Israelite assembly had asked Moses to send the spies. When the spies returned, they made their report to the whole assembly as well. In retrospect this was probably a mistake. Things may have turned out differently if Moses had had them deliver their report privately.

How thorough were the spies in checking out the land?

> The spies started in the Desert of Zin which is in the Sinai Peninsula and went as far as Lebo Hamath which is in what is now Syria. To do this, they traveled approximately 500 miles in 40 days. This is an average of 12.5 miles per day. Assuming that they rested on the Sabbaths, they would have had to travel about 15 mile per day on the other days. In doing so, they looked over the entire territory God had promised the Israelites. In harmony with the instructions Moses gave them, they not only surveyed the territory, they brought back representative produce from the land.

What was the majority report?

All of the spies acknowledged that the land of Canaan was everything God had promised it would be. Nevertheless, 10 of the 12 men reported that it would be folly to try to invade. They told the assembly, "We can't do it!"

Lesson: That's the whole point! God never intended them to do it in their own strength. In our own strength we are bound to fail. When we rely on God and do what He has told us to do, we can accomplish the impossible.

What reasons did the scouts give for not being able to conquer the land?

> Their response was one of unbelief and fear. They said that the inhabitants were stronger than the Israelites. Not only were they stronger, they were bigger. The spies seemed to have an inferiority complex, "We seemed like grasshoppers in our own eyes…" (Numbers 13:33 NIV)

> In the middle of this litany of woe, the spies said something very curious. They said that the land devoured those living in it. If this was really so, then how come the inhabitants were so big? How come the inhabitants were so powerful? How come the locals hadn't wasted away if the land really was unhealthy? If the land really was toxic then how come the produce was so good, plentiful and large?

Lesson: People often use irrational arguments to justify their own cowardice and unbelief.

What was the reaction of the people to the negative report?

> Instead of recognizing the contradiction in what the scouts reported, the people believed the negative report and reacted with dismay. They wept, they grumbled against Moses and Aaron. They accused God of bringing them all this way only to kill them. They talked about appointing new leaders and going back to Egypt.

III.   Minority Report (Numbers 14:5-10, Deuteronomy 1:29-34)

Two of the scouts brought a minority report which was very different than what the other 10 had said. They did their best to persuade the people that the land of Canaan, instead of devouring its inhabitants, was exceedingly good. In addition, they reminded the people that God was with them and had withdrawn His favor from the Canaanites. There was no need to fear.

What was the people's response to Caleb and Joshua when they said that the land could be conquered?

> Not only did the people reject the message, they turned on the messengers. They talked about stoning Joshua and Caleb. God's intervention prevented this from going beyond just talk.

IV.   God Has The Final Say (Numbers 14:11-38, Deuteronomy 1:34-40)

Our view of a situation and God's view may be very different. The people were looking at giants and their own insignificance. God viewed their attitude as contempt toward Himself. He viewed their threatened actions as unbelief.

What was God's response to the people's rebellion?

> There were several consequences to the contempt and unbelief of the people.
>
> 1) The people had accused God of bringing them to the border of Canaan in order to kill them by the sword. Because of their refusal to enter the land, God threatened to destroy them with a plague.
>
> 2) God promised to make a greater and stronger nation from Moses' descendants.
>
> 3) After Moses persuaded God to spare the Israelites, God made them wander in the wilderness of the Sinai Peninsula for an additional 38 years. In that time, all the people who had refused to enter the Promised Land; all those twenty years old or older, would die. They would die in the desert while their children, whom they had said would be destroyed if they attempted to enter Canaan, would be the ones who would do so. Of the original adults who left Egypt, only Joshua and Caleb would be spared.

How did Moses get God to relent from destroying the people?

> Moses pointed out that if God destroyed the people, it would reflect badly on His reputation. The surrounding nations and the Egyptians would say that God had been unable to fulfill His promises. On the surface it would look like God was being arbitrary – He couldn't do what He promised, so He disposed of the people.

What happened to the men who made the negative report?

> God struck them down with a plague.

Lesson: It never pays to bad-mouth God's plan. It never pays to discourage people from following God's plan. When we decide that we know better than God, we will often suffer the very consequences that we thought we would avoid by disobeying what God has told us to do.

V.   Better Late Than Never? (Numbers 14:39-45, Deuteronomy 1:41-46)

When the people realized the consequences of listening to the negative report, what did they attempt to do?

> After God had pronounced judgment on the people, they acknowledged their sin and mourned bitterly. Unfortunately, they also decided that they were going to do what God had told them to do originally. God commanded them to turn back toward the desert along the route to the Red Sea. (In this case, "Red Sea" probably refers to the Gulf of Aqaba. It's a translation of the Hebrew term *Yam Suph*, which literally means "Sea of Reeds." In other passages, *Yam Suph* almost certainly indicates other bodies of water such as the Gulf of Suez.) Instead, the people decided that they would conquer Canaan after all.

What was the result of their action?

> Moses warned them not to try it. To try to conquer Canaan at this stage would only be another act of disobedience. God was not with them. Because God was not with them, they

would not succeed but would be defeated by the Canaanites. As usual, the people refused to listen and went ahead with their plan. As Moses predicted, they were badly defeated.

Lesson: Sin destroys opportunities. Repentance does not erase consequences. To try to avoid the consequences only compounds the problem. The way to avoid the consequences of sin is to refrain from sinning in the first place.

శాుస

Revolt in the Desert
(Numbers 15:32-36, 16:1-17:13)

Introduction: Because of their refusal to enter the Promised Land, God condemned the Israelites to an additional 38 years in the wilderness. During those years the entire generation which had refused to obey God's command to conquer the land, except for Caleb and Joshua, would die out. Unfortunately, even after they suffered the consequences of disobedience, the spirit of rebellion was still there.

I.   The Sabbath Breaker (Numbers 15:32-36)

One form of rebellion manifested itself by showing contempt for the Covenant laws God had given the nation. A man was caught gathering firewood on the Sabbath instead of resting.

What is the Sabbath?

> The Sabbath was the seventh day of the week, that is Saturday. God created the universe and all the plants, animals and man during the six days of creation. Then, He rested from His creative work on the seventh day.

What was the big deal about breaking the Sabbath?

> One of the Ten Commandments was to keep the Sabbath holy (Exodus 20:8-11). The Sabbath was not only a reminder of God's rest after His creative work, it also was a symbol of the promise God had given the Israelites to take them into the Promised Land. In comparison to the slavery they had endured in Egypt and the wanderings in the wilderness, going into the land was pictured as a rest. (Compare Numbers 14:23 and Deuteronomy 1:35 with Psalm 95:11.) The person who decided to work on that day was deliberately thumbing his nose at God.

What was the penalty for breaking the Sabbath?

> The Law was very clear. Anyone who violated the Sabbath by doing work on it was to be put to death (Exodus 31:14-15,

35:2). Apparently, the man who gathered wood on the Sabbath thought he was above the Law – it didn't apply to him – God didn't really mean what He said. It seems a very strange attitude to have after witnessing all God had done, and all the times He had already demonstrated that He meant what He said.

Lesson: There are still a lot of people who think that God doesn't mean what He says in Scripture, or that the warnings don't apply to them. It's a very dangerous mindset to have. God does keep His word. He does not make exceptions. Sooner or later, the consequences of our actions will catch up to us.

Tangent: Some people call Sunday the Christian Sabbath. Is it? Do Christians have a Sabbath? While it makes perfect sense to rest from work at least one day a week, in the New Covenant there is no command to do so or to treat any day differently than any other. (See Romans 14:5-6, Galatians 4:10-11.) Christ has fulfilled the Law. The New Covenant is not based on law but on the sacrifice of Christ. If we are in Christ, we are free from rules and regulations like the Sabbath law. While Christians assemble on the Lord's Day, that is Sunday, in order to remember Christ, hear the Apostles' teaching and to encourage, exhort and comfort one another, the Lord's Day is not a Sabbath. It is perfectly permissible to do anything on the Lord's Day, including work, which is permissible on any other day. In the New Covenant our Sabbath rest is being with God and Christ in the new heaven and earth. (See Hebrews 3:14-4:11, 2 Peter 3:13.)

II.   Rebels With A Cause (Numbers 16:1-50)

While the situation with the man gathering wood was an isolated, personal affair, the next instance of rebellion was far more serious. It threatened the established order of things. Korah, Dathan and Abiram issued a direct challenge to Moses' and Aaron's leadership.

What was the beef of Korah and his associates?

> They claimed that Moses and Aaron had given themselves their positions of leadership (Numbers 16:3). Since the entire community was holy, then they had just as much right to lead

as Moses and Aaron did. This is quite similar to the complaint that Miriam and Aaron had made against Moses in Numbers 12. In this case, Korah and his fellow Levites weren't content with their role of serving in the Tabernacle and wanted a shot at the priesthood which was reserved for Aaron and his descendants.

What was the accusation made by Dathan and Abiram? (Numbers 16:12-14)

1) You've taken us out of a land flowing with milk and honey to kill us in the desert.

2) You lord it over us.

3) You haven't brought us to a land flowing with milk and honey.

4) You'll gouge out our eyes if we answer your summons.

How do you evaluate the complaints these men made?

They were a total distortion of history.

1) While Egypt certainly offered a different and more diverse diet than was available to the Israelites during their time in the wilderness, Dathan and Abiram seem to have forgotten what Egypt was like. The truth was that they were slaves and had had to work at hard labor for the food they got. If Egypt was really so wonderful, why had they left?

2) Moses and Aaron had not appointed themselves. God had put them into their positions of leadership. Instead of lording it over the Israelites, Moses had interceded for them time after time in order to spare them from God's wrath.

3) In reality, Moses had led them to the border of the Promised Land, flowing with milk and honey. It wasn't Moses' or Aaron's fault that the people had refused to enter. Moses and Aaron, both, had torn their clothes when the people threatened to choose new leaders and return to Egypt rather than enter Canaan (Numbers 14:5).

4) Whatever faults Moses and Aaron had, cruelty was not one of them. Whatever punishments Moses had handed out were according to the Covenant Law which God had given. Far from being vindictive or cruel, Moses had time after time pleaded with God to forgive the people for their trespasses.

Lesson: We need to make sure that we don't exaggerate and distort the truth. Make sure that our complaints are legitimate and based on fact. Most of the time when we look back at the "Good Old Days" we forget the real conditions. Our minds filter out the bad things and the pain we experienced then. We compare the hardships and troubles of today to the good of the previous times.

What test did Moses suggest to demonstrate who God had chosen as the priests?

> Everyone was to bring a censor of incense before the Lord. The Lord would demonstrate who the real priests were. Incidentally, it shows just how serious the rebellion was that these people had provided themselves with censors. Who but a priest would have had one? They must have been very certain that they would be able to take the preisthood over if they had gone to the trouble of making censors.

> There should have been no need for anyone to demonstrate who the real priests were because God had already said who were to be the priests. However, for some people God's word is not enough. They won't believe until God shows His power visibly. The problem is that by that time it is often too late for the doubters.

What was God's response to the situation?

> The tents and households of the guilty were swallowed up in a fissure. The false priests were burned up by fire.

What was the reaction of the rest of the community when they saw God's judgment?

> They blamed Moses and Aaron. They accused them of destroying the Lord's people (Numbers 16:14). How incredibly ironic since it was Moses and Aaron who had pleaded for the

people! (Numbers 16:22) Further, it was not Moses' or Aaron's doing, but God who destroyed Korah and the false priests.

What did God do?

He sent a plague among the people. 14,700 additional people died.

Lesson: When we associate ourselves with people who rebel against God, we will suffer the same consequences as they do.

How did God reaffirm Aaron's position as priest? (Numbers 17:1-13)

The leader of each tribe was to bring his staff. The staffs were then placed before the Lord in the Tabernacle. Aaron's staff blossomed and produced almonds. The other staffs didn't. This finally put an end to all the grumbling and complaining about who was supposed to be the High Priest.

Tangent: What are the duties of priests?

1) To offer sacrifices

2) To pray on behalf of others

3) To tell others God's word

In the church age, who are God's priests?

Every Christian is a priest (1 Peter 2:4-10). We, too, have a responsibility to perform the duties of priests:

1) Offer sacrifices (1 Peter 2:5, Romans 12:1, Hebrews 13:15-16)

2) Pray (Ephesians 6:18, 1 Timothy 2:1-4)

3) Tell others (1 Peter 2:9, 3:15-16)

෧෨

The End In Sight
(Numbers 20:1-21:35)

Introduction: Because of their refusal to enter the Promised Land when God brought them to it, God sentenced the Israelites to another 38 years of wandering in the deserts of the Sinai peninsula. With two exceptions, all those 20 years old and older would die in the wilderness. It would be their children – the ones they were afraid would die in the attempt to conquer Canaan who would be the ones to enter in.

There is little recorded about those 38 years. Presumably, they were years of monotony in which nothing much happened. When we get to Numbers, chapter 20, the time of waiting was drawing to a close. Unfortunately, the period of time just before a long stretch of waiting comes to an end can be the hardest to bear. The Israelites experienced a few more tragedies and disappointments before they were finally able to receive the promise God had made to them so long ago.

I.   Two Strikes And You're Out (Numbers 20:1-13)

No matter how long we've been with the Lord; no matter how faithful we've been, we must never let down our spiritual guard. If we get complacent or neglect to renew our relationship with God on a continual basis, we set ourselves up for a fall. We still face temptation. We can still allow our natural tendencies to overrule our spiritual training. This is what happened to Moses on the verge of finally entering the land God had promised.

As you look over Moses' career to this point, what was his greatest weakness?

> Moses had a tendency to act impetuously. His actions were often driven by anger.

> Exodus 2:11-12 His impulsive killing of an Egyptian taskmaster led to his having to flee from Egypt.

Exodus 2:17 The flip side of acting impulsively is the ability to take decisive action. Moses' coming to the rescue of the shepherdesses led to his obtaining a wife.

Exodus 11:8 Moses lost his cool with Pharaoh.

Exodus 16:20 Moses got angry with people who didn't obey the instructions about collecting manna.

Exodus 32:19 Moses got angry when he saw the golden calf Aaron had made at Mt. Sinai and he broke the stone tablets which had the Ten Commandments written on them.

Leviticus 10:16-20 Moses lashed out at his brother instead of making allowances for Aaron's grief at losing two sons.

Exodus 16:15-22 Moses became angry when his integrity was called into question and asked God not to accept the offerings of his accusers. Right after that, Moses had to appeal on behalf of the entire community.

Though the text does not explicitly say that Moses was angry when he struck the rock, his words certainly imply that he was. Because of his impulsive action in striking the rock instead of just speaking to it like God had commanded, Moses was banned from entering the Promised Land.

Lesson: We need to learn to control our passions and emotions so that they don't drive us to do things or say things that we will regret later. Paul wrote this about himself. "...I beat my body and make it my slave so that after I have preached to others, I myself will not be disqualified for the prize." (1 Corinthians 9:2 NIV)

Tangent: Is all anger wrong?

No. Anger, in itself is not a sin. God, Himself, becomes angry. But, we must be very careful to not let our anger lead us into sin. ""In your anger do not sin": Do not let the sun go down while you are still angry, and do not give the devil a foothold." (Ephesians 4:26-27 NIV)

If anger is not sin; if anger is even a part of God's character, then why is it so dangerous? James writes, "My dear brothers, take note of this: Everyone should be quick to listen, slow to speak and slow to become angry, for man's anger does not bring about the righteous life that God desires." (James 1:19-20 NIV) The key difference which we need to understand between God's anger and ours is that God's anger is always an extension or an expression of His righteousness. All too often our anger is an expression of unrighteousness. God's anger is ignited by wrongdoing or injustice. Our anger is often a reaction to something which we feel has been done against us.

II.   The Priest Must Die (Numbers 20:22-29)

God had said that everyone over 20, with the exception of Joshua and Caleb, would have to die before the Israelites could enter the land. Numbers 20, verse 1, recorded that Moses' sister Miriam had already died. Aaron had to die too. This meant that his role of high priest had to be transferred to someone else. Eliazar, Aaron's son, was appointed to take his place.

III.   The Reward Of Impatience (Numbers 21:4-9)

It's hard to wait. It's particularly hard to wait when the end is in sight. When you've been waiting a long time, even little things can become big irritations. Sometimes it's the little things which are hardest to deal with. Remember that these people had been waiting for 38 years to get to go to their destination. When Edom refused to let them pass through their territory, it must have been very frustrating and discouraging. We're so close, yet so far from reaching our destination!

What did the people do when they lost patience?

As usual, they started complaining. They complained about having left Egypt.

What should their response have been?

> "My brethren, count it all joy when you fall into various trials, knowing that the testing of your faith produces patience. But let patience have its perfect work, that you may be perfect and complete, lacking nothing." (James 1:2-4 NIV)

What was God's response when the people voiced their frustration?

> He sent venomous snakes among them.

What was the cure?

> They had to look at the bronze snake Moses hung on a pole.

Application: Jesus used this incident as a foreshadowing of His own crucifixion (John 3:14-18). There are a number of parallels between the two incidents.

> 1) Just as God provided a way to be saved from the snake-bite, He has provided a way to be saved from sin.
>
> 2) Salvation is not automatic. A person had to look at the bronze snake to be cured from a bite. Today, a person has to take part in the new birth, which Jesus' death on the cross makes possible, in order to be saved from sin.
>
> 3) A person wouldn't look at the snake unless he had faith that doing so would cure him. Similarly, a person won't experience the new birth unless he has faith in Jesus.

Question: To whom or what are we looking for our salvation?

IV.   Responses to Hostility (Numbers 20:14-21, 21:1-3, 21:21-35)

The march to the borders of the promised land was not made without opposition. The Israelites encountered three, similar yet distinct types of conflict. What were they?

> 1) The refusal of the Edomites to let them pass. The people of Edom were descendants of Jacob's brother Esau. In other

words, they were related to the Israelites. Permission to go through their territory would shorten the journey the Israelites would have to make in order to reach the Jordan River. Edom refused and threatened war if the Israelites came through their territory.

What was the Israelite's reaction to the refusal?

> They went around Edom's territory and bypassed it.

2) The Canaanite king of Arad attacked the Israelites and captured some of them. What was Israel's reaction?

> Keep in mind that this king and his people were among those whom God had instructed the Israelites to destroy. It is significant that even though this territory was part of the land promised to the Israelites, they still asked God's blessing before they retaliated against the wrong which had been done to them.

3) The Amorite kings refused passage and mobilized their armies against Israel. How did the Israelites respond?

> They fought and destroyed these kings and their people. In contrast to Edom, the Israelites could not bypass this territory in order to get to their goal. They either had to go through this land, or give up trying to get to the Jordan River.

Lesson: Avoid conflict if possible. But, do not let conflict keep you from accomplishing what God has told you to do. Do not act on your own but seek God's leading in how to handle conflict and confrontation. If we do what God has told us to do in the way God has told us to do it, then we can count on God's blessing. "Do not repay anyone evil for evil. Be careful to do what is right in the eyes of everybody. If it is possible, as far as it depends on you, live at peace with everyone. Do not take revenge, my friends, but leave room for God's wrath, for it is written: "It is mine to avenge; I will repay," says the Lord. On the contrary: "If your enemy is hungry, feed him; if he is thirsty, give him something to drink. In doing this, you will heap burning coals on his head." Do not be overcome by evil, but overcome evil with good." (Romans 12:17-21 NIV)

&⚬℘

The Donkey and the Seer
(Numbers 22:1-41)

Introduction: Originally, it had not been the Israelites' intention to conquer or occupy any of the territory east of the Jordan River. God had promised them only the land of Canaan. It was only when the the peoples east of the Jordan, specifically the kings Sihon and Og, refused them passage and mustered their armies against them that the Israelites conquered their territory. When Edom had refused passage, the Israelites had bypassed their territory. But they could not bypass the territory of Sihon (the Amorites) in order to arrive at the approaches to Canaan, opposite of Jericho. The resulting fight left the Israelites in possession of all the land east of the Jordan from the top of the Dead Sea to the northern border of Bashan.

The land to the east of the Dead Sea belonged to the Moabites and Midianites.

I.   An Unreasonable Fear (Numbers 22:1-4)

Who were the Moabites?

> They were descendants of Lot, Abraham's nephew. (See Genesis 19:36-37.) They were the Israelite's relatives.

Who were the Midianites?

> These people were descended from Abraham through his wife Keturah. (See Genesis 25:1-4.) That being the case, these people were even closer relatives to the Israelites than the Moabites. In fact, Moses wife, Zipporah, was from Midian (Exodus 2:15-22).

Did the Moabites have reason to fear the Israelites?

> No, they did not.

> 1) They were relatives.

> 2) They didn't live in the territory God had promised to the Israelites.

3) The Israelites had deliberately bypassed their territory to avoid conflict.

4) God had specifically told the Israelites not to bother the Moabites (Deuteronomy 2:9).

Lesson: Before we act, we need to make sure that our fears are reasonable. We need to make sure that we have the true facts. Moab didn't need to feel any threat from Israel. The Israelites had already gone out of their way to avoid trespassing on Moabite land. But because Balak and the other leaders gave in to their unreasonable fears, they set a chain of events into motion which were to have tragic consequences not only for Israel, but themselves as well.

II.   Answering The Call (Numbers 22:4-20)

What did the Moabites do?

> They sent for Balaam to put a curse on the Israelites. Balaam was a Seer (that is a prophet) who lived up by the Euphrates River.

What was Balaam's reply?

> He inquired of God. When God told him that the Israelites were blessed and that Balaam was not to curse them, Balaam sent the Moabite ambassadors away.

What was Moab's next move after Balaam refused to come?

> They upped the ante. They promised a larger reward.

How did Balaam respond to the new offer?

> He said that since God had refused permission, he couldn't go no matter how much money he was offered. But he also said that he would talk to God again about it.

What's wrong with this picture?

> God had already told Balaam what the situation was and what his response ought to be. Since God had already made His will clear, why was there any need for anything more to

be said? Obviously, Balaam was hoping that God would change His mind. The Apostle Peter points out that Balaam's basic problem was that he was greedy. He put a higher priority on money and position than he did on truth and serving God (2 Peter 2:15-16).

Lesson: When we already know God's will, there's no need to ask Him what His will is. To do so indicates that we have wrong motives and sin in our hearts. It's fine to ask God how to implement His will. It's fine to ask how His will applies in a particular circumstance. It's fine to ask if we're confused about His will. But if we know His will, then we had better obey instead of asking God to change His mind.

If God didn't want Balaam to go, why did He give permission?

Perhaps for several reasons:

1) God will often help us along the path we've chosen – even if it's a wrong path. For example, if we deliberately turn our backs on the truth because we love falsehood, God will make sure that we are handed a great big lie to believe (see 2 Thessalonians 2:10b-12).

2) The sin had already been committed. By allowing Balaam to go ahead, God would give him several opportunities to recognize what he was doing and repent of it.

3) Though there would be tragic consequences from Balaam's sin, God would use him to also bring great blessing to the Israelites through the prophecies he was going to speak.

III.   Who Is The Bigger Donkey? (Numbers 22:21-35)

What was God's reaction when Balaam left for Moab?

He sent the Angel of the Lord to oppose him with a drawn sword. When Balaam's donkey saw this, she turned away from the danger three times. Ironically, the donkey could see more than this person who was supposed to be a Seer.

How did Balaam treat his donkey?

> The donkey spared Balaam from death, but Balaam beat her
> for her trouble. There are several ironies in this scene.
> Balaam is after wealth and prestige. He so consumed by it
> that he isn't even startled when his donkey talks to him. He
> blames the donkey for making him look a fool. He doesn't
> realize that he really is one. He says that he'd kill the donkey
> if he had a sword. He doesn't realize that there really is a
> sword near by – and it's the donkey which has spared him
> from it. The donkey has always been faithful – looking out
> for the best interests of her master. It is the master who is
> being unfaithful, both to the donkey and, especially, to God.

Lesson: We need to be sensitive to spiritual realities. What we view
as perversity may actually be what spares us from calamity. The
problems we encounter may be God's attempt to wake us up and to
get us to repent.

What would our animals say to us if they could talk? Would they
expose our inconsistencies and sin? Do we treat them unjustly?

Was Balaam sincere in his confession that he had sinned? What sin
was he confessing?

> It's unclear what Balaam was actually confessing. It's
> possible that he was acknowledging that he was wrong to
> beat his donkey. From his next statement, however, it seems
> that he might be acknowledging that he shouldn't have
> started on the journey. Regardless, his statement that he will
> go back if God is displeased shows what is really in his heart.
> He wants to go on. God couldn't have made it any plainer
> that He didn't want Balaam to go to Moab. He had said so
> right at the first. When Balaam went anyway, God had
> blocked the way three times. Now Balaam is asking whether
> God is displeased?!

Lesson: We shouldn't think that confessing sin gives us a license to
go on with it. Just because God permits something doesn't mean that
He's pleased with it. Confession should always be accompanied by

repentance. We must not just acknowledge it, but actually turn away from the wrong that we've done.

IV.   Trying To Ride The Fence (Numbers 22:36-41)

God had made His displeasure with Balaam very plain. But Balaam still wanted the reward from Moab. So, he tried to ride the fence. He tried to please both the king of Moab and God. On the one hand, he said that he could only say what God told him to. On the other hand, he participated in the sacrifices Balak made.

Lesson: We can't have it both ways. If we are going to serve God, then we can't participate in anything which is contrary to God's purposes. "Therefore, my dear friends, flee from idolatry. I speak to sensible people; judge for yourselves what I say. Is not the cup of thanksgiving for which we give thanks a participation in the blood of Christ? And is not the bread that we break a participation in the body of Christ? Because there is one loaf, we, who are many, are one body, for we all partake of the one loaf. Consider the people of Israel: Do not those who eat the sacrifices participate in the altar? Do I mean then that a sacrifice offered to an idol is anything, or that an idol is anything? No, but the sacrifices of pagans are offered to demons, not to God, and I do not want you to be participants with demons. You cannot drink the cup of the Lord and the cup of demons too; you cannot have a part in both the Lord's table and the table of demons. Are we trying to arouse the Lord's jealousy? Are we stronger than he? (1 Corinthians 10:14-22 NIV)

ಐಛ

Blessings and Curses
(Numbers 23:1-25:18)

Introduction: In spite of God's instructions and warnings, Balaam answered the king of Moab's summons to come and curse the Israelites. It was clear that his priority was prestige and financial gain rather than serving God. Though tragedy resulted, God also used this false prophet to bless His people.

The prophecies Balaam spoke are worth studying in detail. However, we are only going to look at some of the highlights.

I.   A Separate People (Numbers 23:1-12)

What was the dilemma Balaam faced when he tried to curse the Israelites?

> God had already blessed these people. Since God is the supreme ruler, no one can overturn what He has already decreed. No curse or denunciation can stick when God has said otherwise.

What was different about the Israelites? What made it possible for God to bless them above other people?

> They considered themselves a people apart from other nations. They deliberately chose to be different than other peoples.

Lesson: The followers of Christ are also to be different from the people around them. Though Christians are in the world, they are not to be of the world (John 17:14-16). To say it another way, they are not supposed to have the same values and priorities that the world has. They are to think differently (Romans 12:2). Christians are to separate themselves from the world (2 Corinthians 6:14-18).

What wish did Balaam express?

> Upon realizing that the Israelites were under God's blessing, he said that he also wanted to be counted as righteous. He hoped to experience the same kind of end or death as they.

Lesson: The only way to die the death of the righteous is to live the life of the righteous. Balaam wanted the blessing while still living according to his own desires. Similarly, there are a lot of people who want the benefits of being in Christ without the responsibility. They want the reward of the righteous while living like the world. They view Christ as a fire insurance policy. They view God's grace as a license to sin. It doesn't work that way. The only way to obtain the blessings and promises is to die to self and live for Christ (Matthew 16:24-27).

II.   A Comparison (Numbers 23:13-26)

Balaam's second oracle emphasizes the contrast between him and God.

What are the characteristics of God?

> God does not lie. He does not change His mind. He fulfills what He says.

What is the result for the people of Israel?

> No one can change God's blessing. They do not suffer misfortune. They have God's strength. No sorcery or divination can be used against them. God works through them.

How does Balaam's character compare with God's?

> Though it is not directly stated, the text implies and the context makes plain that Balaam's character is the opposite of God's. Balaam changed his mind about going to Moab. Balaam could not fulfill his intention to curse Israel. He has resorted to sorcery and divination to try to counter God's blessing (see Numbers 24:1).

III.   A Greater King (Numbers 23:27-24:14)

Upon realizing that God had determined to bless Israel, Balaam gave up trying to reverse the blessing by using sorcery or divination. He probably realized, for the first time, that God could not be manipulated. Instead, it was God who manipulated him – in each of the two oracles Balaam spoke, the text says that God put a message in his mouth (Numbers 23:5, 23:16). Balaam still wanted to curse Israel and earn the reward Balak had promised him, but he realized that his usual methods wouldn't work. This time however, God's Spirit came upon him.

There are two special points to notice in Balaam's third oracle.

Numbers 24:7 says that their (the Israelites') king will be greater than Agag. Who is Agag?

> Agag was the king of the Amalekite people during the reign of King Saul of Israel several hundred years in the future. This is an amazing case of prophecy. Hundreds of years before it happened, Balaam predicted that a king of the Israelites (long before the Israelites even had a king) would be greater than the king of another nation. This prophecy came true when God commanded Saul to destroy the Amalekites. Saul captured Agag and the prophet Samuel executed him. (See 1 Samuel 15.)

> Because Saul did not fully obey God's command, many Amalekites survived. This became an important factor later on during the time of Queen Esther. Hamaan, the man who tried to wipe out the Jews, was a descendant of Agag. His motive for trying to destroy the Jews was apparently to take revenge for what Saul had done. Hamaan's wife seems to have been aware of Balaam's prophecy when she told Hamaan that he would come to ruin (Esther 7:13).

Another remarkable part of Balaam's third oracle is in Numbers 24:9. There Balaam says that those who bless the Israelites will be blessed while those who curse them will be cursed. With these words, Balaam is really bringing a curse upon his own head, and that of Balak who had hired him, by attempting to curse Israel. Unfortunately, Balaam seems not have believed his own prophecy. As we shall see, he continued to try to bring a curse on the Israelites and, in so doing, brought about his own destruction.

Lesson: God's word is true, whether we like what it says or not. We need to learn to embrace it wholeheartedly rather than resisting it or rejecting it.

V.   Prophetic Warnings (Numbers 24:15-25)

Balak was naturally very upset that his scheme to curse Israel had backfired so badly. He fired Balaam and refused the reward he had promised. Before leaving, however, Balaam spoke some more prophecies. We will take the time to only mention one of the remarkable things he said.

Numbers 24:17 mentions a star which would rise and a scepter which would come out of Jacob. A star is metaphor for an important and prominent person. A scepter, of course, refers to someone who rules. So, in this prophecy Balaam predicted that there would be an extremely important ruler among the descendants of Jacob – that is Israel. This is a prediction of the coming of Christ. Among His titles is "Morning Star" (2 Peter 1:19, Revelation 22:16). Jesus has also been anointed "King of Kings" (Acts 2:36, Philippians 2:9-11, Revelation 19:16).

V.   Roundabout Curse (Numbers 25:1-18)

At first it might seem like there is no connection between the events of Numbers, chapter 25 and Balaam's oracles. However, there is a profound connection. The events of chapter 25 are a logical progression from Balaam's attempt to curse Israel.

What did the Israelite men begin to do?

> They started to indulge in sexual immorality with Moabite women. This was not merely about sex. The sexual behavior was directly linked to the worship of the Moabite gods. Sex acts were part of the worship. The men were turning away from God and becoming involved in the corrupt practices of the Moabite nation.

How did God tell Moses to deal with the situation?

> God instructed Moses to kill the ringleaders and expose their bodies. No doubt the reason for such drastic action is that if the situation wasn't dealt with, it would have destroyed the community.

> **Application:** The principle of taking public action against leaders is carried into the New Testament. "Do not entertain an accusation against an elder unless it is brought by two or three witnesses. Those who sin are to be rebuked publicly, so that the others may take warning." (1 Timothy 5:19-20 NIV)

What was it that stirred Phinehas to action?

> A prominent Israelite man brought his sex partner into the camp in full view of everyone. The Hebrew is a little ambiguous in describing what happened. Some commentators feel that this couple were having sex in worship of false gods right in the Tabernacle itself! In any case, regardless of where the act took place, it was done in open and brazen defiance of the Israelites' covenant with God. Such conduct not only broke the covenant but, if left unchecked, would destroy the Israelite's status as a separate and blessed people. It could not be ignored.

How did this whole episode come about, anyway?

> It was Balaam who suggested the whole scheme. He failed when he tried to curse Israel, but he figured out how to bring the Israelites under God's curse. (See Numbers 31:15-16, Revelation 2:14.)

Lesson: No one can take us away from God. No one can bring us under a curse when God has blessed us. But, we can walk away from God's blessings. We can turn our backs on God and bring ourselves under His curse. Jesus said, "My sheep listen to my voice; I know them, and they follow me. I give them eternal life, and they shall never perish; no one can snatch them out of my hand. My Father, who has given them to me, is greater than all; no one can snatch them out of my Father's hand." (John 10:27-29 NIV) Peter writes,

"But in keeping with his promise we are looking forward to a new heaven and a new earth, the home of righteousness. So then, dear friends, since you are looking forward to this, make every effort to be found spotless, blameless and at peace with him. Bear in mind that our Lord's patience means salvation, just as our dear brother Paul also wrote you with the wisdom that God gave him. He writes the same way in all his letters, speaking in them of these matters. His letters contain some things that are hard to understand, which ignorant and unstable people distort, as they do the other Scriptures, to their own destruction. Therefore, dear friends, since you already know this, be on your guard so that you may not be carried away by the error of lawless men and fall from your secure position." (2 Peter 3:13-17 NIV)

VI.   Aftermath

There were several important consequences of this episode.

1) The plague God sent as a result of the sexual misconduct was stopped as a result of Phinehas' action, but 24,000 people had already died.

2) God made a covenant with Phinehas and his descendants.

3) God declared the Midianites (the nationality of the woman Phinehas killed), enemies. At God's direction the Israelites sent an armed force against the Midianites and killed all the males and every girl or woman who was not a virgin (Numbers 31:1-18). Presumably, the reason the virgins were spared is that they had not been involved in worship of the false gods. Remember that sex was an integral part of that worship.

4) The Moabites were prohibited from becoming part of the Lord's community for ten generations. The Israelites were never to seek friendship with them (Deuteronomy 23:3-6).

5) Balaam was killed (Numbers 31:8). The man who expressed the desire to die the death of the righteous, died as an unrighteous man. The man who put personal gain ahead of serving God, never got to enjoy whatever reward was given

him for cursing Israel. "What good is it for a man to gain the whole world, and yet lose or forfeit his very self?" (Luke 9:25 NIV)

৪৩৩

Appendix – Thoughts on the Exodus

Some events are so dramatic, or so traumatic, that they forever imprint themselves on a nation's psyche. The Exodus was such an event. It was something which forever changed the Israelites. The Old Testament writings mention it scores of times – probably more than any other event. Not only that, the prophets over and over again quote God describing Himself as the One who brought the Israelites out of Egypt. Even if the Israelites had been inclined to forget the Exodus, their yearly observance of the feast of Passover would have reminded them of it.

The Timing Of The Exodus

It should be obvious that something which had such a profound effect on the Israelite people must have had its base in an actual historical event. Yet some people do question whether the Exodus actually happened. Leaving aside those who do so out of an anti-biblical or anti-Jewish bias, the major reason for discounting the Exodus seems to be the date at which it is supposed to have occurred. Critics say that the events of the Exodus and the subsequent conquest of Canaan simply do not conform to what is known from other sources. According to them it does not fit either the written sources in Egypt or the archaeological discoveries in Canaan.

However, it turns out that the assertions of the critics are based on an assumption regarding the dating of Egyptian history. There is an argument about when some of the Pharaohs reigned. The controversy is far beyond the scope of this essay. In short, if one accepts the later dating, then the events of the Exodus and the conquest of Canaan could not have happened as the Bible describes them. On the other hand, if one accepts the earlier dating then the archaeological record matches the biblical account amazingly well.

Aside from my faith in the inspiration and inerrancy of Scripture, the clinching argument for me about which dating method is correct, and therefore the historical accuracy of the Exodus, is the form of the covenant God made with the Israelites at Mt. Sinai. Ancient covenant documents followed different forms and conventions during different times of history. As I mentioned in Lesson 7, *Covenant Codified*, the "Law of Moses" follows a pattern which is found only during a relatively narrow time-period. This period was from 1,400 through 1,200, that is, the second millennium B.C. Covenants on either side of this period are quite different. To me this seems decisive evidence that those who hold to a late date for the Exodus are wrong. Recognizing the correct time-period of the giving of the Law also brings the extra-biblical evidence into harmony with the biblical record. (For an in-depth discussion of these points, see Kitchen, K.A., *On the Reliability of the Old Testament*, William B. Eerdman Publishing Co., 2003.)

The Route Of The Exodus

There has also been a lot of discussion about which route the Israelites took when they left Egypt. There are three proposals: a northern route along the coast of the Mediterranean Sea, a route through the middle of the Sinai Peninsula, and a southern route along the the east coast of the Gulf of Suez.

Obviously, we must base our decision on which route is most likely, solidly on the biblical account. If a particular route does not harmonize with what the record says, it cannot be correct. Conversely, if we insist that the biblical descriptions of the route are inaccurate, why should we believe anything else Scripture says? In that case it all comes down to personal preference.

The Northern Route

The only reason to consider this route at all is that some modern commentaries suggest it. Also, the maps in the back of some Bibles show it as a possibility. However, there are two things which make it almost certain that the Israelites did not travel towards the Mediterranean.

The first is that Exodus 13:17-18 specifically states that God did not allow the Israelites to take the northern road which went from Egypt to Philistine territory. In spite of the fact that the Israelites left Egypt armed for battle, they were not yet capable of facing the warfare which would have inevitably resulted from trying to enter Canaan from that direction.

The second reason to rule out the northern route is that it led right through an Egyptian militarized zone. There were a whole string of forts along the road. The Israelites would have had strong Egyptian forces in front of them as well as behind them as they fled bondage. Nowhere does the account indicate that the Israelites encountered an Egyptian army in front of them. On the contrary, Exodus 14:9-10 clearly states that the Egyptians overtook them from behind.

The Middle Route

In recent years a growing number of people have suggested that the Israelites marched through the middle of the Sinai Peninsula. The reason for this suggestion is that they speculate that Mt. Sinai, where God entered into covenant relationship with the Israelites, is actually located east of the Gulf of Aqaba in what is now Saudi Arabia, instead of the "traditional" view which places Mt. Sinai in the southern portion of the Sinai Peninsula. If this is so, it follows that the crossing of the Sea took place somewhere on the Gulf of Aqaba. This, in turn, implies the Israelites traveled through the middle of the Sinai in order to reach the Gulf.

One reason for placing Mt. Sinai to the east of the Gulf of Aqaba is Paul's statement in Galatians 4:25 in which he says that Mt. Sinai is located in Arabia. However, we can't just project modern political boundaries back into ancient history. Paul was a citizen of the Roman Empire and was writing to people who lived in the Roman Empire. We have to interpret what he said in light of the geopolitical realities of his time. The Romans equated the Arabs to the Nabateans and at the time Paul wrote, the Nabateans (Arabs to the Romans) controlled the entire Sinai Peninsula except for a narrow strip along the Mediterranean which connected Egypt to Palestine. In other words, at the time Paul wrote, Sinai was part of Arabia and we cannot take his statement as proof that Mt. Sinai was located on the east side of the Gulf of Aqaba.

In addition, there are several other geographical realities which argue against the middle route. For one thing, Scripture seems to indicate that the Israelites left Egyptian territory when they crossed the Sea. That is, until they crossed the Sea, they were still within the boundaries of Egypt. However, Egyptian territory never extended as far as the Gulf of Aqaba.

In Exodus 14:2 God tells the Israelites to camp near Pi Hahiroth, between Migdol and the sea. Those who place Mt. Sinai in Saudi Arabia try to locate Migdol and Pi Hahiroth on or near the Gulf of Aqaba. Yet, Jeremiah 44:1 places Migdol in Northern Egypt. Ezekiel 29:10 implies the same. Therefore the theory seems to contradict plain statements of Scripture.

Exodus 15:22 says that immediately after crossing the sea, the Israelites went into the Desert of Shur. Genesis 16:7-14 implies that Shur is in the upper part of the Sinai Peninsula. Genesis 20:1 makes this even plainer. Genesis 25:18 states that Shur was near the border of Egypt. Based on these statements, wherever the crossing took place, it had to have been somewhere well to the north of the Gulf of Aqaba.

Exodus 16:1 relates that the Israelites came to the Desert of Sin 15 days after leaving Egypt and, therefore, 15 days after the crossing. There is no doubt that this desert is in the Sinai Peninsula. Therefore, the crossing must have taken place to the north.

Similarly, Exodus 19:2 and Numbers 33:15 state that the Israelites came to the Desert of Sinai. There is no question that this desert is in the lower part of the peninsula. It is definitely not on the east side of the Gulf of Aqaba. Also note, that the Israelites got there after crossing the sea! The obvious conclusion is that the crossing had to have taken place well to the north.

Again, after the events at Sinai, Numbers 33:36 says the Israelites moved on from Ezion Geber to Kadesh in the Desert of Zin. This places them on the west side of the Gulf of Aqaba.

There is another reason to discount the possibility of the Israelites taking the middle route through the Sinai Peninsula: logistics. Exodus 14:7 says that Pharaoh mustered 600 of his best (NIV) chariots for the pursuit, along with *all* the other chariots of Egypt. The text does not tell us how many chariots Egypt had, yet it seems safe to say that the number chariots characterized as "best" would have been a small sub-set of the total. Even assuming parity in numbers between the "best" and the "rest", there would have been a minimum of 1,200 chariots in the pursuit. Each chariot carried two men, an archer in addition to the driver. An additional four men were assigned to each chariot. At least one provided support on foot. No doubt the others provided maintenance and looked after the horses. Assuming a total of 1,200 chariots, there were 7,200 men in the force.

Aside from the six men assigned to each, Egyptian chariots required two horses to pull them. This means that 2,400 chariot horses were present.

In addition to the chariots, Exodus 14:9 explains that cavalry and infantry were also part of the force. How many men does this represent? We cannot know for certain. However, Egyptian doctrine called for chariots to shield or screen the infantry. Chariots were divided into squadrons of 25. Infantry was composed of regiments of 200 men each. Presumably there was one chariot squadron per infantry regiment. Assuming this is correct, we can extrapolate the number of infantry in the pursuing force. There were 48 squadrons of chariots. At a one-to-one ratio, there would have also been 48 infantry regiments totaling 9,600 men. We have no way to estimate how many cavalrymen and mounts were attached to the force in addition to the infantry.

Since foot-soldiers are not specifically mentioned in Exodus as being among those who drowned, it is tempting to conjecture that the chariots and cavalry had out-distanced them by the time they tried to cross the Sea. However, Isaiah 43:17 clearly implies that the infantry was also caught up in the disaster. What are the implications? A combined force can only move at the rate of its slowest component. If the infantry was destroyed along with the chariots and cavalry, it means that the entire force traveled at the pace of the infantry. Egyptian infantry could travel an average of 15 miles per day. The straight-line distance from Egypt to Aqaba is about 150 miles. The actual distance the army would have had to travel is much longer. In any case, assuming the Israelites took the middle route through

Sinai, it would have taken an absolute minimum of ten days of forced marches for the Egyptian army to catch up to them at the Gulf. (For a fuller description of chariot warfare see, Richard Carney, *The Chariot: A Weapon that Revolutionized Egyptian Warfare.*)

Now think what this means in terms of supply. Each man needed 3 pounds of wheat or its equivalent per day to meet minimum calorie requirements. Each man also needed a minimum of 9 quarts (two and a quarter gallons) of water per day. This means the Egyptian expeditionary force needed 252 tons of wheat and 378,000 gallons of water just to reach the Gulf. This does not include the needs of the cavalrymen. Nor does it include the tons of fodder and the hundreds of thousands of gallons of water needed for all those horses.

Normally, many of the needs of a chariot or cavalry force can be met by foraging along the way, but the route through the middle of the Sinai is arid and barren. There is almost no water, and there is little greenery and no agricultural crops upon which the horses could feed. Even if there were, the Israelite flocks and herds would already have consumed much of what was available. Not only that, the force was moving away from its base of supply. Nor could the Egyptians count on being resupplied upon reaching their destination as they could if they had been marching toward Canaan. Remember also that this was a hasty deployment. There was no time for the Egyptian host to establish advance supply dumps. (As an aside, did you ever wonder why Joseph needed to send carts to move a family of nomads to Egypt (Genesis 45:19-27)? The most likely reason was so they could haul enough fodder and water to keep their flocks alive as they traveled through the arid wasteland between Canaan and Egypt.)

But it gets worse. The whole point of the expedition was to bring the Israelites and their herds and flocks back. Even if the Egyptians could have reached the Gulf in 10 days, they would have been limited to the pace of the herds and flocks on the way back. Further, they would have been traveling back over territory that had already been grazed out – assuming there had been anything to graze to begin with. In other words, in addition to their own requirements, the Egyptians would have had to transport enough fodder and water to support huge numbers of animals for at least two weeks. Not to mention the provisions needed for all the people they were bringing back.

How likely is this? Not very. Scripture indicates that the Israelites were only able to carry enough supplies to keep themselves going for about three days. (See Exodus 15:22 and Numbers 10:33-11:1.) It's highly doubtful that the Egyptians could have brought along enough provisions to meet their own needs, let alone enough extra to meet those of the Israelites for the weeks needed to take them back to Egypt.

There is still another reason to doubt the middle route. The wadis leading from the interior of the Sinai down to the Gulf of Aqaba are rough and narrow. Assuming that chariots could negotiate them at all, they could have only done so on a narrow front. It would have been relatively easy for defenders to trap and defeat a chariot force in detail. This is not the picture the account in Exodus gives.

The Southern Route

The southern route has the Israelites traveling down the eastern side of the Gulf of Suez. About halfway down the Gulf they turned to the southeast toward Mt. Sinai which is located in the southern part of the Sinai Peninsula.

Aside from the process of elimination is there anything to recommend the southern route? There is. The Hebrew text of Exodus 15:4 indicates that the Egyptians drowned in (and therefore the Israelites crossed) the *Yam Suph*, or "Sea of Reeds." After leaving the *Yam Suph* (Exodus 15:22), the Israelites traveled into the desert. Eventually, they came to Elim with its 70 palm trees (Exodus 15:27). Numbers 33:10 states that after leaving Elim the Israelites camped on the shore of the *Yam Suph*.

So, after having crossed the Sea and traveling away from Egypt for several days, the Israelites camped by the Sea again. The logical conclusion is that the body of water near which they camped is the Gulf of Suez (Red Sea). There isn't another body of water which fits the narrative.

Not only does the Gulf of Suez match the narrative, there is nothing else in the narrative which would eliminate the southern route. Though some of the locations of the places mentioned are speculative, they are more reasonable than the suggestions made for the other routes.

The Location Of The Crossing

Given that the southern route is the only logical one for the Israelites to have taken, the next question is where they crossed the Sea. There are two possibilities. We cannot say with certainty which of them is more probable. Unfortunately, the excavation of the Suez canal probably disturbed or destroyed a lot of archaeological evidence which might have helped answer the question.

The first possibility for the crossing is somewhere in the lakes region between the Gulf of Suez and the Mediterranean. After crossing, the Israelites would have marched through the desert to the east of the lakes.

The second possibility is that the Israelites marched down the western side of the lakes until they were trapped at the northwestern tip of the Gulf of Suez. They crossed through the tip of the Gulf and headed southeast into the desert.

Stephen gives this second possibility oblique support in his speech to the Sanhedrin. He says that the Israelites left Egypt at the Red Sea (Acts 7:36). The writer of Hebrews also says that the people passed through the Red Sea (Hebrews 11:29). However, it is possible that the Red Sea extended further north in Moses' day than it does now. It is even possible that the lakes which are north of the Gulf were once part of it. Therefore we cannot take the statements in the New Testament as definitive proof that the second possible crossing site is the correct one.

The Miracles Of The Exodus

Miracles are an essential part of the Exodus narrative. They are what make the Exodus so distinctive and unique. Throughout mankind's

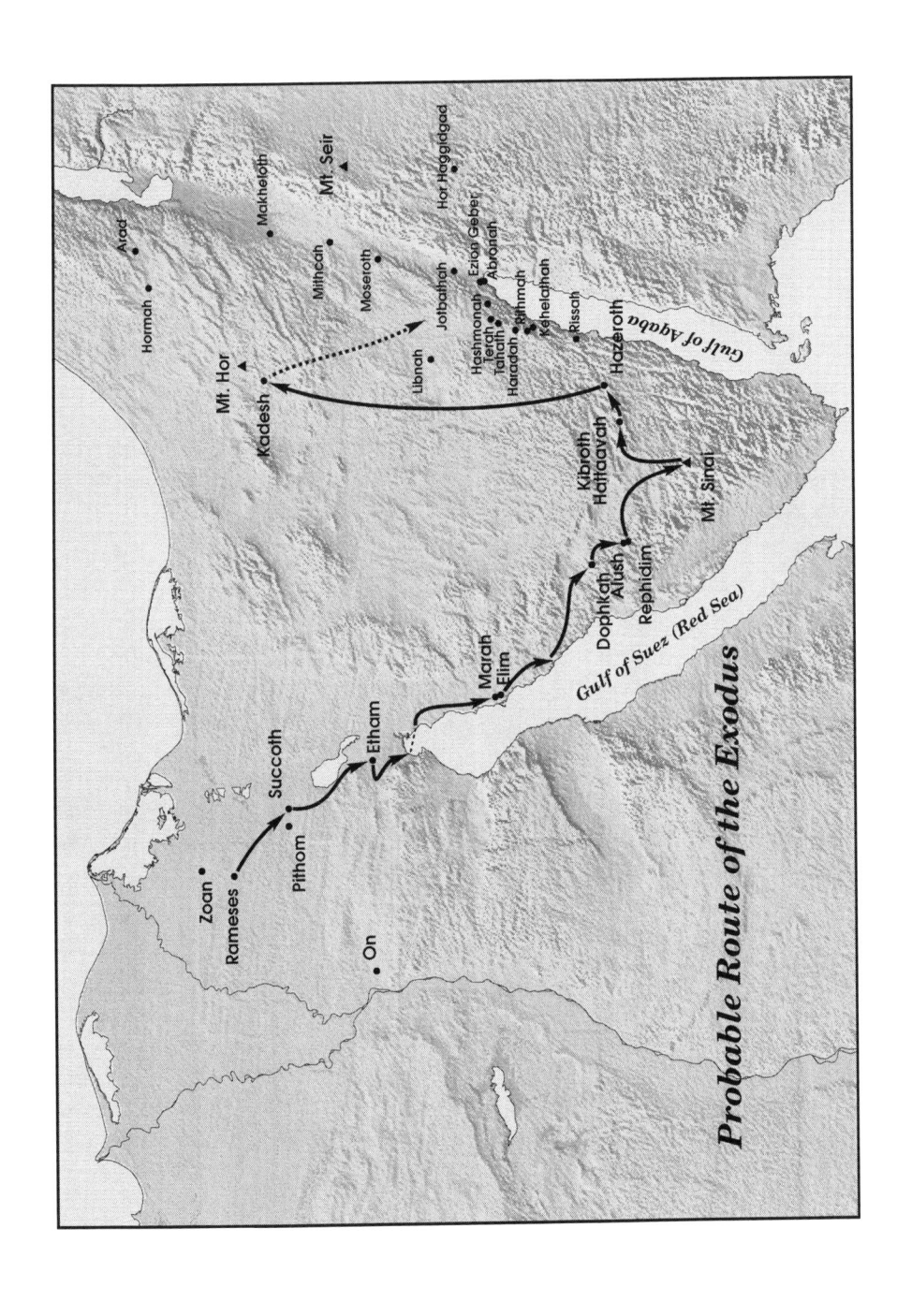

Probable Route of the Exodus

long history there have been many migrations. None of them are as steeped in the supernatural as the Exodus.

However, the miracles of the Exodus are far more than God's intervention on behalf of the Israelites. They have a profound spiritual significance. The Plagues were not merely a series of supernatural diseases which paved the way for Israel's expulsion from Egypt. They were a demonstration of God's power (Exodus 6:1), they were judgments on the gods of Egypt (Exodus 6:6, 7:4, 12:12) and through them the Egyptians would recognize who God is (Exodus 7:5, 9:14). The blood of the Passover lamb was not merely a talisman which kept the Israelite first-born from dying. It was a tangible reminder of God's redeeming grace (Exodus 6:6, 13:14-16) and an anticipation of a greater redemption to come (1 Corinthians 5:7-8). The crossing was not merely a convenient way to get out of Egypt without battle. Through it the Israelites were not only delivered from slavery but mystically joined to Moses (1 Corinthians 10:2). The crossing also foreshadowed water baptism through which people today are freed from sin and joined to Christ (Romans 6:3-7). The manna was more than a supernatural provision of food. It represented something more significant, that is, God's Word (Deuteronomy 8:3). It also pointed to God's Word made flesh in Christ (John 6:32-58).

Because of the spiritual significance of the Exodus miracles we must be careful not to minimize them. Commentators like to speculate on possible natural phenomena behind the miracles. They point out that many of the plagues could be explained in terms of things already common in Egypt, writ large. For example, they will say that the plague of frogs is just a wild increase in the frog population which already inhabited the Nile. Similarly, hail is not unknown in Egypt. The plague was merely an unusually heavy storm. They speculate that the drying up of the Sea so the Israelites could cross might somehow be tied to the eruption of the volcano Thera in the Mediterranean. The route the Israelites took through the wilderness happens to parallel the migratory path of quail, etc.

No doubt, nature is not divorced from the miracles of the Exodus. The Bible itself points out some of the linkages. For example,

Exodus 14:21 says, "…all that night the Lord drove the sea back with a strong east wind and turned it into dry land…" (NIV) But we must not make the fatal mistake of seeking a purely natural explanation for every miracle. Nor do possible natural elements in an event preclude it from being a miracle. As C.S. Lewis pointed out, nature and miracles are not mutually exclusive. Even when God is the direct cause of a particular event, the effects of His action often follow the natural order. (See C.S. Lewis, *Miracles, A Preliminary Study*, Macmillan Publishing Co., 1978)

To remove the supernatural from the Exodus (or, for that matter, any of the other miracles recorded in the Bible) is to miss the transcendence of God. To diminish the miracles removes one of the very purposes of the Exodus, "…I am the LORD, and I will bring you out from under the yoke of the Egyptians. I will free you from being slaves to them, and I will redeem you with an outstretched arm and with mighty acts of judgment. I will take you as my own people, and I will be your God. Then you will know that I am the LORD your God, who brought you out from under the yoke of the Egyptians." (Exodus 6:6-7 NIV)

ஐ൦൫

Bibliography

Ash, Anthony L. and Cottrell, Jack, Editors, *College Press NIV Commentary*, College Press, various volumes

Carney, Richard, *The Chariot: A Weapon that Revolutionized Egyptian Warfare*, http://historymatters.appstate.edu

Dean, B.S., *An Outline of Bible History*, The Standard Publishing Company, 1912

Gaebelein, Frank E., General Editor, *The Expositor's Bible Commentary with the NIV*, Zondervan, various volumes

Kitchen, K.A., *On the Reliability of the Old Testament*, William B. Eerdman Publishing Co., 2003

Lewis, C.S., *Miracles, A Preliminary Study*, Macmillan Publishing Co., 1978

Pritchard, James A., Editor, *The Ancient Near East, An Anthology of Texts and Pictures*, Princeton University Press, Volume I, 1958, Volume II, 1978

Sarna, Nahum M., *Exploring Exodus, The Heritage Of Biblical Israel*, Schocken Books, 1986

Smith, Malcolm, *The Power of the Blood Covenant*, Harrison House, 2002

Smith, Mont W., *What the Bible Says About Covenant*, College Press Publishing Co., 1981

ଽୠଔ

About the Author

Jonathan Turner is both a preacher's kid and a missionary's kid. He grew up in Pakistan where his parents served as church planters. He came to his own faith in Christ through their influence and example.

In addition to writing and teaching, Jonathan is actively involved in carrying on the mission work his parents began. He has also served as an Elder at the congregation he attends.

Jonathan and his wife have been happily married for over 30 years. They live in Oregon and have two grown children who are also in the Lord.

You can view some of Jonathan's musings on the church and other aspects of life in Christ at:

www.presbyterjon.com

೫◌ಐ

Made in the USA
San Bernardino, CA
18 June 2014